CULTURE SHOCK!

SUCCESSFUL LIVING ABROAD

A Wife's Guide

Graphic Arts Center Publishing Company
Portland, Oregon

In the same series

Argentina	Egypt	Laos	Sri Lanka
Australia	Finland	Malaysia	Sweden
Austria	France	Mauritius	Switzerland
Belgium	Germany	Mexico	Syria
Bolivia	Greece	Morocco	Taiwan
Borneo	Hong Kong	Myanmar	Thailand
Britain	Hungary	Nepal	Turkey
California	India	Netherlands	UAE
Canada	Indonesia	Norway	Ukraine
Chile	Iran	Pakistan	USA
China	Ireland	Philippines	USA—The South
Cuba	Israel	Scotland	Venezuela
Czech Republic	Italy	Singapore	Vietnam
Denmark	Japan	South Africa	
Ecuador	Korea	Spain	

Barcelona At Your Door	New York At Your Door	A Student's Guide
Chicago At Your Door	Paris At Your Door	A Traveler's Medical
Havana At Your Door	Rome At Your Door	Guide
Jakarta At Your Door	San Francisco At Your Door	A Wife's Guide
Kuala Lumpur, Malaysia		Living and Working
At Your Door	A Globe-Trotter's Guide	Abroad
London At Your Door	A Parent's Guide	Working Holidays
		Abroad

Illustrations by Shirley Eu-Wong
Cover photographs from Image Bank

© 1992 Times Editions Pte Ltd
© 2000 Times Media Private Limited
Revised 2001
Reprinted 1996, 1998

This book is published by special
arrangement with Times Editions Pte Ltd
Times Centre, 1 New Industrial Road, Singapore 536196
International Standard Book Number 1-55868-646-0
Graphic Arts Center Publishing Company
P.O. Box 10306 • Portland, Oregon 97296-0306 • (503) 226-2402

Printed in Singapore

*To Rodney, Lilly and Jamie for
all their love and support; and,
to traveling wives everywhere
for their inspiration.*

CONTENTS

PREFACE

A decade has passed since *A Wife's Guide* was first published. Then, it was almost revolutionary, if not slightly radical, for a book to recognize the needs of the accompanying expatriate spouse.

Now, things are changing. Many companies are introducing pre-departure training and in-country support programs to help the expatriate employee family. Increasingly, not only wives, but husbands or same sex partners accompany their spouses.

The biggest change in the world over the last decade must be technology. With the Internet, an expatriate spouse now need never feel cut off from receiving the latest news from home or friends who have moved on. Even children would have no problems keeping in touch with his home curricula and friends.

Internet helps to cushion the culture shock of a new home as numerous expatriate websites offer country information and on-line support. Even local produce is readily available on-line and working from halfway around the globe is possible. Some companies are also starting to secure work permits for their expatriate employee's spouse.

It's funny how the more things change, the more they remain the same. Accompanying spouses now are still experiencing the same problems their predecessors faced ten years ago—raising third-culture children, professional adjustments, loneliness, repatriation shock. At the end of the day, perseverance and flexibility will still be the vital elements that will help a spouse succeed in this fast-paced society.

The first step toward hurdling past these challenges would be to recognize them and support will come in the following pages.

Always remember that there will be some tough days at the beginning for an overseas assignment, but they will be overwhelmingly outnumbered by many more wondrous days of learning about a whole new environment. Knowing what challenges lie in store, managing one's expectations and keeping them grounded in reality will ultimately pay off in the end.

—Introduction—

EXOTIC RUTS

It's easy to picture her standing at a cocktail party in some distant land, respectably dressed, sipping from a glass, and smiling at some foreign official with whom she's smoothly engaged in polite conversation. More likely, the image you have of her is from a television newscast, where she steps off an emergency evacuation flight in the middle of the night, baby in one arm and toddler clinging to the other, looking like she just came through a war (which she may well have done).

Who is she? She's the international traveling wife. Instead of moving to the next state or province, she moves every few years from one side of the world to the other. Married to a foreign service, a multinational corporation, a bank, a newspaper, a church, or merely a small export business, she is the ultimate portable wife and probably a mother too. Her career is mobile, her makeup duty-free. She can say 'please' and 'thank you' in several languages and knows how to evaluate a school or a servant in thirty seconds. In the wake of a husband's career, her life – and the lives of her husband and children – seem to effortlessly glide from one exotic outpost to another. She's the backbone of the international family, the emotional rock. She's also the last person anybody really thinks about until all the clean underwear runs out.

Behind that friendly facade of competence and sociability there often lurks one very scared, emotionally exhausted, and in many cases angry 'accompanying' wife. On good days, she can easily extol the virtues of an overseas assignment, not the least of which is the romance and adventure of life in a foreign culture. She loves watching her children grow up in an international setting, attending schools which brag about the high number of nationalities the way an ice cream parlor promotes its flavors.

But talk to her on a bad day, perhaps while she seems to be sipping demurely from that glass at a reception, and you'll discover she is in actual fact irritated beyond words to have been forced to attend her third reception of the week, only to engage in the same pointless small talk she's made thousands of times before in other countries to officials who couldn't care less about her other than that she's Mrs. Husband's Job.

"And how are you enjoying our country?" the official asks her wherever she is in the world.

"I'm so glad we moved here," she will lie. "The people are so warm and friendly that I just love it here already," she'll say, drinking quickly so as not to choke on her own hypocrisy. On that day, it may just so happen, far from being caught up in the romance of a new assignment, she was in the throes of the hostility common to the early adjustment period. Instead of warm and friendly, she found the locals intrusive, rude, and stupid. She wants to go home.

"It's been so easy settling in," she may continue, all the while remembering the ancient dirt and grime which coated her apartment walls and the countless phone calls to non-existent numbers on a broken phone, in a futile search for good domestic help or a grocer who operates a delivery service.

"I am so happy to hear that," the official will lie back to her. These foreign women have it so good, he thinks. Rich bitches.

His transparent cultural resentment will go unnoticed. She's too busy thinking how she struggled through an hour's worth of congested traffic just to stand there drinking on an empty stomach while back at her apartment, her children are probably working over the new baby-sitter who keeps giving in to their every whim despite her clear instructions.

At the other end of the room stands the angst-ridden neophyte to expatriate life, the one who wonders how a woman like herself from a small town ended up clutching a sweaty glass, her third one mind you in the past twenty minutes, because some wandering waiter keeps zeroing in on her, forcing her to drink more than she knows she should.

Am I dressed properly? she is asking herself for the thousandth time. Why don't I look as relaxed as the woman standing over there with that foreign official? Oh no, he's coming over here now. She gulps.

"And how are you enjoying our country?" she is asked.

"Excuse me?"

"How are you enjoying our country?"

"I'm terribly sorry, but I can't seem to understand what you are saying."

Is he speaking English?

"HOW...ARE...YOU...LIKING....MY....COUNTRY?" he says, wondering how soon he can go home to his own wife, who is not always invited – and perhaps just as well – to these functions.

"Oh, of course, your COUNTRY. It's very nice. The

people are so nice, too. It's so nice to be here." Help me, she screams.

She glances over to a wife engaged in a heated discussion with a pin-striped man.

"So why can't I work here?" she overhears the woman saying.

"You can work here."

"I'm not a secretary and I don't want to stamp visas. I'm a journalist and I want to work as one. Is that so unreasonable?" she is demanding to know.

"I've told you many times, dear. That one's not up to me," a man, obviously her husband, replies, wearily.

"Then why don't I ask *him*?" she says, pointing to the official. There, that ought to wipe that patronizing grin off your face, she thinks.

"Please don't do that, dear," he warns, trying to ward off a diplomatic incident.

"And how do you like our country?"

I'd like it a lot better if you would let me work here, the former career woman is thinking but instead holds her smile as tightly as her glass and says: "Oh, it's just lovely here. Excuse me, please, I'll leave you men alone to chat."

Stupid sow, thinks the official. Won't even talk to me.

Today's traveling wife could be any one of those women – or all of them at the same time. She willingly (more or less) agreed to follow her husband on his overseas assignment because the thought of foreign adventure sounded intriguing when explained to her around her kitchen table back home. The sound of all those opportunities to travel, the allure of different domestic set-ups, the cost of living allowances to compensate for her dropping out of the work force, in short, a golden neo-colonial lifestyle, it all sounded exotic as could be and an escape from the rut she had clearly dug herself into at home.

Instead, here she is in a new routine, with a different backdrop which certainly is exotic, but is also so confusing and alien she can't even figure out where to buy the toothpicks she forgot to put into her shipment.

Her children are taken care of and she can't figure out how on earth to fill her time, especially if the local authorities won't let her work at her own profession. Worse still, she's expected to learn to play bridge, tennis and golf, speak the local language fluently, and find a dressmaker to create a local sensation for her to wear to something called the Marine Ball in three weeks' time. What on earth is a Marine Ball?

She's an emotional mess and this might not even be her first time overseas. Why wasn't it like this last time? she may wonder. Oh, right. I didn't have kids then; or, I was pregnant; or, my children were still babies; or, my husband was still in a junior position and I saw him more, and on and on.

Even if you have never personally met any of these traveling wives, you have likely heard of a friend who has a friend who every few years mails off hundreds of new change of address cards bearing still another foreign postmark. Her stories, even heard second-hand, always sound exciting. There's no lack of stimulation in her life.

True enough. But there's more to this story than meets the eye. If you are about to become one of these traveling wives yourself, or are considering it and can't decide if the idea excites you or depresses you, there a few things you need to know before you take the plunge.

For those women repeating the experience, you may want to reacquaint yourself with the emotional hurdles you have to cross over yet again.

I hope you will find some of the advice contained within these pages useful. Too many women are being sent overseas with little or no adequate preparation to help guide them through the emotional transition from life at home to life abroad.

A healthy state of mind is critical if a woman is to fashion a new life which is a satisfying and rewarding experience – for her, as well as for her family.

It's not enough to just learn about the practicalities of renting a house, shipping a dog with the lamp shades, or finding new schools for the children. A woman needs reassurance that she's not losing her mind because she is fearful about day-to-day life in a new culture. She needs to know that it's totally normal to feel exhausted in the first few months and that other newly-arrived women also want to do nothing all day but sit around and read trashy, escapist novels instead of joining a club or meeting new people.

She especially needs to know that on some days it's OK to feel like she can't stand herself, can't face her own image in the mirror, hates her hair, her body, and most of all, her husband for dragging her halfway around the world to watch her own self-esteem plummet, her sense of identity vanish in the new time zone, and her self-confidence get thrown away with the empty moving boxes.

She's not the first woman – nor will she be the last – to watch her emotions do battle while her sense of self-worth gets up and walks away.

Most important of all, she needs to know that life does return to normal, and after experiencing the ultimate crisis of confidence, she will become – and feel like – herself again. Only there will be much more to her.

A woman simply can't move around the world, live in an alien culture, learn how to adapt, raise her children, make new friends and travel as much as possible just for starters, without becoming a more fascinating person, with experience which contributes to opinions and stories worth listening to. She simply will never be the same again.

Why am I qualified to hand out advice on this subject? Over a fifteen-year period, beginning with our first assignment to Bangkok and followed by diplomatic postings to Taipei, Beijing and Seoul (with re-entries to Canada in between, finally ending up in Vancouver, British Columbia where I hope to never see another moving box), I have been fortunate to have experienced the life from expat to repat.

My daughter was born in a Bangkok hospital operating room by Caesarean section. I was attended by an oversupply of nurses, who seemed like midgets compared to the nine pound two ounce girl who was mercifully removed from me in a surreal birthing sequence I doubt Franz Kafka could describe. My pregnancy was a miserable experience, compounded by the worst case of culture shock, since my daughter arrived in Bangkok nine months and two weeks after my husband and I did. Nobody advised me it might have been wise to wait a few months to allow myself the time to make the countless adjustments to a new life overseas. In fact, nobody advised me of much of anything, which is why I decided in the first place to write this book and follow it up with its companion, *Culture Shock! A Parent's Guide*.

Since the first edition of this book, technology—and in particular e-mail and the Internet—has changed expatriate life dramatically for the better. Accompanying spouses can now receive more support (both emotional and practical) than ever before. Shopping can be done over the Internet; friends and family can remain in touch via e-mail; careers are more easily pursued and maintained thanks to the virtual world; and expatriate web sites (like my own at http://www. expatexpert.com and others) have created on-line expatriate communities, allowing families to find both support and comfort in the knowledge that everyone faces similar challenges no matter where they are in the world.

But information delivered over a computer or even in the pages of a book will never replace the human contact spouses desperately need when they first arrive in an unfamiliar place and begin the process of reinventing their lives. For that reason, throughout these pages you will repeatedly find me recommending support groups of all descriptions. No one knows our experiences as well we do; no one is better equipped to help a new spouse better than another one. Remember that you are not alone, neither in your reactions and feelings to your new life, nor in the wonderful cultural experiences you are privileged to enjoy.

What makes a good traveling wife? More than anything else, it is the ability to keep laughing, even when you want to lock the bathroom door and not come out until the assignment is over. If you do lock yourself in, though, please take this book along with you. You will discover that you are not alone and that in all probability, despite the ups and downs of the early months of adaptation, you will want to come out again and live life to the fullest in your new surroundings.

Chapter One

Understanding Pre-Moving Day Jitters
Due to Circumstances Beyond Your Control

Just weeks before our departure to Taiwan for my husband's second overseas assignment, all hell broke loose in Beijing's Tiananmen Square. The Chinese government, which was thought to be encouraging a more enlightened political era, chose instead to open fire on democracy and kill many of the young people who had been demonstrating for such an ideal. China plunged backwards into repression and martial law.

The unexpected bloodshed in the Chinese capital became the media event of the month. Hyped-up news specials screamed from the television screens. The story took up entire newscasts. Elaborate video graphics flashed out the message – China in crisis – China on the verge of civil war. They might just as well have screamed *Don't Go There!*

Overnight, everyone was a China expert. Rarely was the prognosis optimistic – even from the real Sinophiles – at least not in the short term.

It was this short term which particularly concerned me. My husband's job as a foreign service officer was taking us and our two young children – our then two-year-old son and six-year-old daughter – first to Taiwan for one year of Mandarin Chinese language training. Following that, we would take up residence in Beijing for a two-year assignment. By my calculations, the short-term period everybody was so pessimistic about, would roughly cover the years we would spend living on the mainland.

As if my pre-departure anxiety over the Far East wasn't bad enough, it was then further fueled by television coverage of an equally graphic news event which coincided with the China turmoil. From Iran, came horrifying footage of the funeral of the Ayatollah Khomeini. Thanks once again to satellite technology, the world could watch millions of distraught Iranian men banging their fists against their heads in a show of mourning, mobbing their spiritual leader's coffin, and forcing it to open and the body lying within it to fall to the ground.

"Sorry, dear, but I'm not moving anywhere," I informed my husband as we shut off the television after another particularly unnerving newscast. "The world is too fluid. It's a mess."

"Relax," said my husband knowledgeably, always the quintessential unflappable diplomat. "The world's always been a mess. We can just watch the mess now on television. Especially in China. There's been far worse going on there. Nothing's different."

"Far worse? You really know how to reassure a woman."

"You know what I mean. You're a big girl. You've traveled a lot."

"I don't want to be a big girl! There's no way I am taking my children out into that big bad world, especially to the Far East. You can go on this assignment alone." Of course I ended up going. I'm neither cool nor unflappable and together we're living proof of the attraction of opposites. But I fell in love with a man who fell in love with traveling around the world. I chose to become a traveling wife.

LIFE CAN BE DANGEROUS AT HOME

An international crisis is not the greatest prelude to a foreign assignment, especially if it's in the country you're headed for. But for the purpose of getting yourself going, it's wise to bear in mind that life can be dangerous anywhere: you don't have to travel to find it. Statistically speaking, for instance, I have a better chance of dying in a highway accident since studies consistently show driving to be a lot less safe than flying or traveling in general.

It's true that some people thrive on danger, so to them, a world crisis or disaster makes for more adventurous travel. They enjoy the shock value of telling friends they're off to a war zone. However, the majority of people – especially wives and mothers – don't particularly want danger included in the package. As a former news reporter, though, I know that the news reports we watch and read, while they may be accurate, do not always tell the entire truth. Things often look worse from a distance. It is a fact of expatriate life that as a short-term resident of a foreign country, you will likely be unaffected by internal events.

Still, the threat of danger should not be part of the package, and in my own case, I certainly reminded my husband enough of this fact, probably too much for his liking. I couldn't help voicing my worries over and over again. The danger element of traveling, not the exotic lifestyle which supposedly lay ahead, was prominent in my thoughts, my dreams, my nightmares, my everyday consciousness.

HIDING YOUR FEARS

If you're afraid about going overseas, don't be ashamed to admit it. You may not want to take out an advertisement in a major newspaper about it, but I believe the days of solid-like-a-brick British wives have vanished along with colonialism. The rules have changed: you're now allowed to let your emotions surface. Go ahead, be real.

Being an emotional type myself, I am incapable of acting blasé about danger. I will continue in the face of it if I have to, but my eyes will always give away my terror, unless I am around my children and desperately trying not to transfer my fears onto them. In those instances I could win an Academy Award for best performance by a mother concealing her fear. Take the time I had to fly home from our first posting in Bangkok with my then two-year-old daughter: it was one week after an Air India plane which had originated in Canada got blown out of the sky. Only a robot could have boarded a flight to Canada looking unafraid of potential terrorism. But a robot I became after confessing my deepest, darkest fears only to my husband (who naturally had a few fears of his own about sending his wife and daughter off at a time of aviation piracy). My daughter would never have guessed I was afraid, unless she was suspicious of the numerous fancy glasses filled with heavy splashes of a rich alcoholic substance known as brandy which the stewardess fortunately brought me like clockwork once we were airborne. In truth, I wasn't sure what scared me the most: the threat of a terrorist, twenty-four hours in the air with a toddler, or my profound fear of flying even on a bright clear day.

Talking about your fears may not prevent them from materializing. Internalizing them, though, will be another source of stress you could do without.

PREPARING YOUR CHILDREN

When our second Far East assignment drew nearer, and history – televised history that is – was unfolding in Beijing, I recognized that my then six-year-old daughter needed to be briefed about the situation in China. I was worried that her kindergarten school chums might frighten her by repeating what they'd heard their parents say about China. Of course, informing a little girl about the politics of China may sound a bit far-fetched, but it was not completely impossible. I just told her that the Chinese people were a little upset and were wondering about their future, not unlike the way she was wondering what it would be like to move away. I also asked her if anyone had mentioned anything to her about China. She thought my question over for a minute. "You know, Mommy," she said, looking perplexed. "Nobody really cares that I'm moving. Why is that?"

"Well…" I began. Beats me, I thought. It's almost easier to explain calamities or foreign politics to your children, than it is to help them understand their friends' indifferent attitudes towards their pending move. Inadvertently, she was getting her first experience of the way non-traveling families view those who do. "It's kind of an early lesson in life," I answered, only adding to her confusion. She had time enough to learn that as an adult, she will receive similar apathetic reactions from friends.

Instead of politics, it's better to concentrate on your children's emotional well-being by watching for signs of depression or unhappiness, such as sullenness or loss of appetite. Like adults, information is the key to children's readiness for life overseas and it could help them get over any moodiness. Whatever facts you learn through pre-departure briefings, books, or the Internet, share them with your children. Help them find out what they are most interested in knowing by doing a web search of the country you are headed for. Some moving companies now even provide information about the proximity of schools and restaurants.

For younger children, the information you hand out will be slightly different. One of the best reassurances I could give my fearful six-year-old daughter before she would start grade one in Taipei, was the news that just about everyone in her class would also likely be new and not know anybody else. It also helps children get used to the idea of a move, if you let them help with the preparations as much as possible.

Give children of all ages lists of things they can do, like sorting out their toys or clothes. Don't exclude them from packing up. Older children are feeling alienated enough from their friends – don't make them feel like outsiders at home. Younger children want to be part of the action around them. Continually point out the bonuses of moving abroad, like more exotic holidays which you will be able to take as a family. While you're at it, convince yourself of these bonuses at the same time.

EMOTIONAL ROLLER COASTER

In the pre-departure stage, a woman's mood can change several times a day. Before our second time out, no sooner had I got over my immediate hysteria about events in China, when my mood shifted from fear to shame: what kind of person was I to personalize the trauma of the Chinese people?

Was I that shallow and superficial to be so worried about the availability of Cheerios when the fate of a billion people hung in the balance? I was horrified that I could be so self-absorbed, and struggled to find some perspective in my life.

In the end, I managed to convince myself that I couldn't help what I was – a mother and a foreign service wife whose feelings were running wild for very legitimate reasons. I was abandoning all my life props and heading for the great unknown where I would become, once again, an unknown quantity. I had moved abroad before, but this time, I was a different person. I was a parent.

Of course I was concerned about the future of China. But then I was about to travel to Beijing by myself after a home leave in Canada, alone with my two young children because my husband had gone ahead. I'll be perfectly honest about what was uppermost in my mind. It was not ageing Chinese leaders.

Before I actually left Canada for Beijing, a good friend took me to lunch and queried my recent weight loss.

"Deep stress," I answered. "Burns calories."

"Worried about China?" she naturally asked.

"Sure," I replied, "right after I get through worrying about how to put together our hardship shipment of two hundred rolls of toilet paper; finding room in our luggage for all the clothes and toys my family has given the children while we've been home; lugging all that luggage through Vancouver and Hong Kong airports by myself with the kids; surviving the twenty-four hours of flying from here to Beijing without killing myself or them. Should I go on?" I asked. Naturally I hadn't touched the food sitting in front of me.

"So aren't you scared?"

"I'm scared about so many things happening to us that it's all evened out. I'm numb." And not terribly hungry. Wild mood swings from euphoria to feelings of total despair are among the signs that time is running out and moving day is fast approaching. Excitement about the prospect of a new foreign culture is quickly replaced by the anxiety over dealing with the endless details which must be attended to before you can get on the plane. The relief which can come with the thought of getting away from the often petty hassles of family, can turn to sadness that you'll be missing your father's seventieth birthday party. Even the thought of leaving behind your dog can bring a lump to your throat.

You may not be feeling your best either. Unlike the deep stress before my third departure which forced me to alter my clothes, the reverse had happened before we left for the second time. Then, we embarked upon an Endless Farewell Dinner Party, which lasted about two months and added at least five pounds to my waist from too much eating and drinking. My sleep was erratic, and I would awaken long before dawn to mentally add to my list of details for that day. To cope with all my moves and keep my emotions and practical details separate, I resorted to a child's notebook, divided into two simple sections: Things to Do; Things to Buy. I felt in control of something, even if it was only errands.

Feelings of complete distraction and an inability to focus

your thoughts are also completely natural side effects of the anxiety you are feeling. So find something – a book, exercise program, whatever – to give you a temporary escape from all those details.

I was so distracted before our second move, I started renting videos in the afternoon. I even holed up in a darkened movie theater to watch the movie Batman twice in three days. I told my husband it was because I needed a good dose of North American pop culture to keep me going for three years, but when I went out and rented all of Michael 'Batman' Keaton's movies, the pop vision excuse fizzled. I was desperate for diversions, and settled on a dark knight.

There is simply no way around feeling stressed out. It's pre-departure culture shock and no one is exempt, no matter how many times you've moved before. Each move is different (like pregnancies) because the stage of your life, the age of your children, and other human factors will have changed from the last time. If it's your first time out, don't dismiss your overwhelming fear of the unknown. It will color everything.

Physically you haven't left home, but emotionally you're beginning to feel alienated from your friends and family. I knew I had reached my stress threshold when I desperately wanted to smoke a cigarette again after giving them up eleven years earlier. (I won't go into the expatriate 'going back to smoking after quitting for years' phenomenon other than to say I've never tried to quit smoking again so many times in my life). The stress can be from so many different reasons, it's impossible to pinpoint the exact cause. There are the details of selecting a moving company, the nightmare of preparing an inventory of your belongings, closing down your residence, shutting off life in one country to be turned on in the next one. Fear can also feed your stress.

Marital relations are not likely peaking either. On a good day, you think your husband is wonderful for giving you such a fabulous adventure. On a bad day, like the day you have to clean out your garage or basement for your new tenant, you'll want to kill him for getting you into it. (I deal with resentment and anger in Chapter Nine.)

COPING WITH DISASTER SYNDROME

When I first confessed to a friend that I had a horrible fear of losing everyone dear to me overnight, usually by fiery car accident or plane disaster, I was relieved to hear my friend tell me she suffered from the same secret paranoia.

Soon after, I discovered that what I was privately calling 'disaster syndrome', imagining the worst possible scenarios for loved ones, was the so-called mature woman's replacement for adolescent anorexia nervosa. It seemed that all around me, other women were also imagining themselves as widows, childless, and loveless.

This sense of pending doom is heightened when you're about to move abroad, especially if world events run amok. The familiar, safe environment of home is about to be removed and so many new factors over which you have no control enter into the picture. If your children are teenagers, you will likely be worried about the trouble they could get into overseas. If they stay behind, you will still be worried that they are out of your sphere of influence. And what of marriage? Everyone wonders how their marriage will survive the tensions of life abroad, where you can feel literally glued to your spouse financially and emotionally.

And then there's all that flying to get through. As I mentioned, I'm desperately afraid of flying, a condition which I happen to know I share with thousands of other mothers, even if they haven't come right out and confessed to it. Unfortunately, you can't avoid it if you're moving abroad.

On our first posting out, my husband and I were still at the stage where whimsy didn't have to be scheduled, and as a surprise present before we left, he bought me an antique flask which we dubbed my 'flying flask'. I filled it with brandy and would smugly board any aircraft knowing that no matter when the drinks cart would begin its service on board, I could have a good, necessary shot right when I needed it – when the plane rolled down the runway for takeoff.

The second time out, this time with children, I could no longer afford such open indulgence. For one thing, I could not let my children see mommy sneaking a fearful shot, and for another, I needed my wits to be able to take my son to the toilet and not drop him. But around the same time that China was in turmoil and Iranian men were beating their heads in grief, DC10's were once again mysteriously losing their ability to fly. We were scheduled to cross the Pacific in one.

The time had come to do something about my neurotic fear of flying. I had quit smoking with the help of a hypnotist, so I returned for a fear of flying session. As I was going to be in a trance anyway, I asked the hypnotist to see what post-hypnotic suggestions he could leave with me to help my attitude towards moving, my stress, even my inability to learn a foreign language (could I possibly learn Chinese through hypnosis?), and anything else applicable. It more or less worked. Living on the mainland, I could probably use another session to get me through China Air flights.

THERE'S NOT ENOUGH TIME!

I'm not sure who can be ultimately blamed for this particular phenomenon (since nobody will take responsibility) but a move abroad seems always to be announced at the last minute. I don't mean the principle of an international move. You may hear about the idea for months from your husband, whose boss may have mentioned it a few times, or it may come through equally circuitous routes. If your husband is a diplomat, like mine, you know in theory that a move is pending. The question is always twofold: Where are we going? and When will we know for certain?

No matter when the news is finally confirmed, the wife's mind is instantaneously thrown into overdrive. There are a million and one things to get organized and you can't possibly do it all in the time allotted.

If there are teenage children involved, your preparations could be further weighted down by a constant refrain of "You're ruining my life!" which hardly inspires the mental energy you need to get the family into planning the move. Besides which, you may want to turn to that teenager and cry: "What about *my* life?" but your so-called maturity stops you.

When we moved to Bangkok for our first assignment, it was only at the last minute that Thailand was even confirmed as our destination. I had been working on the assumption that we were moving to Jakarta and was busy extolling the virtues of Java and telling people I would send them "care" packages of batik if they were nice to me. Six weeks before we were to move, the location was changed and my head did a somersault in order to sort out the differences between Thailand and Indonesia – which are considerable.

KNOW WHERE YOU'RE GOING

Between the stress and the fear, it's easy to overlook that you are about to move to a brand new country you may barely be capable of pinpointing on a map. As a first step, boot up your computer and find an Internet site that will introduce your children to the new country. It used to be you could buy an atlas, and you still can of course, but the Internet is both atlas and encyclopedia rolled into one and should provide lots of information aimed at children of all ages.

Books can be helpful, but are sometimes out of date or very limited. The best bet is always a human one: find some people who have lived or traveled where you are going. Information will not only be plentiful in the areas you may be interested in, like moving a family, but it will be given to you in a personalized way which is much easier to absorb than dry trade or weather statistics.

Don't be shy about calling up people you've never met, but whose names you've been given. You'll quickly learn that the international community – at home and abroad – are much more receptive to a stranger's phone calls seeking information.

Everyone who moves overseas has been in a similar situation at some point in their moving lives. If you're invited over for a drink or dinner, be sure to accept. Social meetings are as useful as formal briefings. It's also a good idea to begin getting used to meeting new people, as it will definitely be part of your life abroad.

EDUCATE YOURSELF ABOUT SCHOOLS

Information-gathering about schools should follow the same path as the category above. Talk to others who have been to where you're going and to the professionals who may be overseeing your posting. If that doesn't prove satisfactory, call the school directly. A few dollars in long distance will be worth the peace of mind.

Sometimes, general advice can prove useful even if it may not apply to your situation. For instance, before we moved the second time, I had heard from other mothers that skills such as reading and writing were often far more advanced in some international schools than what we were used to at home at a similar grade level.

Since moving was going to be traumatic enough, I didn't want any further surprises for my daughter on the first day of school. Well in advance, we ordered a special series of books which would help her teach herself to read. (*The Cat in the Hat* read-aloud series.) Take no chances. To be forewarned, is to be forearmed.

DECIDING WHAT TO TAKE

I follow a general rule of thumb which someone taught me early on in the game: never take anything precious overseas. Whether it be a baby picture, a family heirloom, or a favorite book, decide if you'd be distraught if it were lost or broken. If the answer is yes, put it into storage or leave it with someone. If you must take it, put it in your purse and carry it on the flight. Similarly, hand-carry any important documents.

If your children are young, try to pack up their rooms in

their entirety, right down to the last stuffed animal. I wish it were possible to physically transport my children's rooms right on the plane, because it would save a lot of grief in waiting to be resettled when you get where you're going.

It's hard to decide just how many sundry items you should load up your shipment with. Often you'll hear that certain items are unavailable where you're going and then find out this isn't the case once you arrive. (We took so much toothpaste to Bangkok, we actually returned home with some three years later.) Take along anything you feel you can't live without, like your special brand of makeup or your children's favorite treats.

OTHER PREPARATORY MEASURES

In keeping with that last bit of advice, I offer a few other pre-departure measures which you may not have thought of:

☛Know How to Use the Internet

Unless you have been living on Mars, this suggestion may sound crazy but there are still people out there who aren't e-mail savvy. Be sure you know how to do e-mail and surf the Internet. Not only will you be able to keep in touch with friends and family, as well as order consumer goods that may not be available in the country you are headed for, you may also want to bookmark your favorite newspaper and magazine sites.

☛Videotapes

While most foreign countries offer video rentals, the shops may not have the particular programs you're dying to watch, or dying for your children to watch. Months ahead of our second assignment, I began taping all the children's shows and movies which I knew we'd need later.

Think of your own needs as well: my husband and I loaded up on episodes of *Star Trek: The Next Generation*. Arrange with a family member – beg if you must – to tape for you while you're away. While we lived in Beijing, the arrival of a videotape could elevate my mood in seconds flat.

Check if there are any censorship laws which may restrict the videotapes you bring in your shipment. Likewise, ensure your video systems are compatible.

☛Change of Address Cards

It's likely you won't know your phone number, but often you do know your new address in advance. You may already have an e-mail address and will in fact be sending notice to everyone via the Internet. Make up an electronic distribution list and copy it onto a diskette, which you may want to hand-carry in your luggage. Never leave home without all your friends' and family's e-mail addresses. Having cards printed up saves you the time of writing out the post office's version over and over again. Your children may get a kick out of handing them around to their friends.

☛Family Portrait

In case you think everyone will forget you, here's a sure-fire way to make sure they don't. Get a friend (it's useful if a friend is a professional photographer) to take a few rolls of film of your family in an informal setting, like the garden or favorite urban hangout. There's bound to be one photo you like. Blow it up and print it before you go and send it with your change of address cards. This especially pleases grandparents.

SAYING GOODBYE

I already mentioned our own Endless Dinner Party which was enjoyable at the time, but cumulatively fattening. The reason we partied on so many different occasions, was so that we could bypass a big blowout where everyone comes, but there's little time to talk with anyone. Smaller parties, with specific guest lists, seemed like a good solution, but I paid the piper in calories. We also seemed to be out all the time, and our children wondered if mommy and daddy had left the country before them. I'm not sure there is any way around an endless round of farewells. My advice is: try eating before you go out so you're not as hungry. When that doesn't work, arrange to get some exercise.

Your children's farewells should be equally as thought-out. You might consider talking with the school about having a cake or small party during school hours. Pay special attention to planning parties for teenage children who may be especially reluctant to leave their friends.

Try to hold something before everyone disappears for the long school holidays. We chose Canada Day for a children's party before we left the second time. It served a dual purpose of reminding the children of their nationality, and it was early enough in the summer so that people were still around. Saying goodbye to parents, especially if they are getting on in their years, is not as easy to plan. They are usually torn between their emotions: they're happy you are leading an adventurous life, but sorry the grandchildren are far away. If they are not well, you will feel the added guilt that you are burdening your siblings with heavier filial responsibilities. Short of canceling your posting, there is nothing you can do to get around leaving unhappy parents, so plan to bring you and your children closer to them through the magic of technology. Home video letters are very popular with grandparents. Invest in a camera and promise to send tapes home on a regular basis so they can see for themselves how everyone is doing. The price of cameras has dropped considerably and may well be worth the emotional investment. Just make sure you buy a camera using the same video system as home.

MEETING THE BOSS AND HIS WIFE

The major goodbye blowout will be with your friends. But before you leave you will also likely have an informal meeting, lunch or dinner, with your husband's boss and his wife (if he is married). Make no mistake, they are checking you out to see how you will represent the company, the government, the product, whatever it is, in a foreign setting.

Most women breeze through this preliminary inspection with flying colors, mostly because they are still on home territory and haven't gone into deep culture shock yet at the other end. (We'll discuss post-arrival meetings with the boss and his wife at your post in another chapter.) Don't worry about this preliminary inspection. You're still excited after all, even if a little frazzled about preparations, but your enthusiasm should save the day for you.

I have learned the hard way to keep my mouth shut during these pre-tour inspections. Mostly I have learned to sublimate my own ego altogether and give no indication (that's if I'm even asked) that I have had a longstanding career of my own and may wish to pursue it on our posting.

If you feel you may come across as some threatening type who is going to be a headache for the boss, the ambassador, or whoever is in charge by demanding better work opportunities, allow me to suggest this: think very carefully before opening your mouth to offer what may be perceived as strong opinions. Overseas, typecasting of wives as strident troublemakers can be instantaneous and long-lasting.

WILLS AND FINANCIAL AFFAIRS

Everyone hates to think of something happening, but don't leave home without making sure your personal affairs are in order.

Not only should you make sure you and your husband have made out your wills, but guardians must be appointed for your children in the unlikely event of an accident. It's horrible to contemplate, but it has to be done, so see your lawyer before you leave the country. This will sound even worse, but make sure your wills cover the possibility that your entire family has an accident.

Financial matters overseas can be one of the biggest headaches you can face. Bank statements are always out of date, and you may run up your biggest phone bill talking to the bank instead of to your family.

One way around such a situation is to hire a professional to see to your affairs while you are away. If you haven't already engaged a professional to look after your house, if you own one, make sure you do so. Never rely on family and friends to see to your affairs. They lead busy lives and may not get around to your affairs as quickly as you'd like. However, there may be occasions when you need to appoint someone (usually a sibling or a close friend) to hold power of attorney so that they will have the authority to sign official documents on your behalf. This is especially important with regard to buying property and selling or renting property which you own.

TO WORK OR NOT TO WORK

Mobile careers and working from overseas is a subject which must be handled separately (see chapter five: Careers Can Travel Too) but in the context of your pre-departure nervousness, my advice is to put work on the back burner.

Your state of panic can only get worse if you start worrying about working too. Give yourself a few months to let the dust settle.

TRAVELING WITH CHILDREN

I've saved this category for last because if your children are young, these will likely be the most elaborate pre-departure

pant...pant... pant!!!

measures you will make, comparable to the battle plans of a general.

Some Airplane Strategies

Booking tickets well in advance is always wise, but if you're traveling with children make sure you book your seats too. These seat assignments should appear on your confirmation computer printout. If you have young movie buffs with you, check to make sure your seats have a view of the movie screen, because there are always a few which don't.

When you tag your hand luggage, make sure you tag your children and everything they are carrying. Put down your name as well, and the airline you are traveling on. It doesn't hurt to add the name of the hotel you will be staying in upon arrival. For some reason, a rumor circulated that the bulkhead seats of an airplane are better with small children. While it's true there may be room to lie them down, or put up a cot for a baby, bulkhead seats are otherwise a nightmare of logistics and should be avoided at all costs.

For one thing, all your hand luggage will have to be stowed above you and will be inaccessible during takeoffs and landings. Tables for games, coloring and eating have to be brought out and attached, and will require assistance from members of the flight crew who may mysteriously disappear for long stretches of time.

A good seating strategy which works if you have two children: divide and conquer. Rather than sit four across where siblings can torture one another, split up into two and two, one behind the other. This way each adult can take on a child individually, and if they go to sleep, it might even be possible for you and your spouse to catch a few minutes of sleep or conversation (but don't count on this).

Mealtime need not be a struggle to get mystery chicken down your children's throats. It's possible to order a special child's meal from most airlines in advance. All it requires is a request and then a reminder as you check in for your flights. Children's meals on some airlines are often better than the regular fare – I devoured my daughter's fresh salad and apple on one flight instead of the usual whipped jello delight offered the adults. A child's meal is often a hamburger and chips which can be a reassuring sight for a youngster. Most airlines also serve the children's meals first, which can be very useful when your child is ravenous or cranky.

But just in case all goes awry with your pre-ordering: always travel with your own emergency food kit of juice boxes (frozen before flight time so they thaw in flight and remain cold), small snacks or raisins, granola bars, miniature cereal boxes or fruit. Especially bring food if you're traveling a no-frills airline like China's or the Soviet Union's. You don't want to see what passes as a snack on some of their flights.

Try to avoid sugary snacks if you want your child to sleep later. One sugary treat though which is a must for takeoff – a bag of sweets. Not only will the swallowing pop their ears, but it works like a pacifier. If you're traveling with a baby and worried about the takeoff, begin feeding, either by breast or bottle, as soon as the pilot begins his roll down the runway.

In-flight crews which are sympathetic to parents are the luck of the draw. Similarly, fellow passengers who don't feel children should be banned from all commercial flights will also be decided by fate.

The other passengers are beyond your jurisdiction, but the flight crew is supposed to be there for you. Don't worry about asking them to heat up a bottle or helping yourself to an extra soda water when your child's been sick. On board a long distance flight, be pushy. If you don't ask, sometimes you just won't receive, and you only hurt yourself by not standing up for the rights you've paid for.

Airsickness – your child's or your own – is something

which has to be endured, like the endless hours of long-distance flying. You can help your children and yourself avoid nausea by eating only light bland foods the day you are traveling. Loading your children's stomachs (or your own for that matter) with gooey, sweet, even spicy, or otherwise dangerous food may not help you when your plane starts bouncing all over the sky in turbulence. Anti-nausea travel medication for adults and children are normally available at drugstores under different brand names depending on where you come from and should be taken before flight time especially if you have a predisposition to airsickness. If all the best laid plans still produce a revolt of the stomach, do not eat anything other than a dry piece of bread or cracker, washed down with ginger ale which has gone flat. If there is continued throwing up, make sure you keep drinking fluids. Dehydration from vomiting is bad at the best of times, but up in the air, breathing airplane air as dry as the Sahara desert can really dry you out.

One final tip on airplanes: if you're flying a long distance flight with toddlers, try to book a night flight if there is one available. This strategy has worked miracles in our family. We took a holiday from Taiwan to Britain and to Spain. Both of the long haul flights between Hong Kong and London and returning (a mere 17 hours in the air) began relatively late at night. It meant we could keep our then toddler son up until flight time, put him in his pajamas as soon as we boarded, bring out his own pillow case for the airplane pillows, and he was asleep before the plane left the runway.

What You Pack is What You Carry
A travel article about packing once appeared in the *New York Times* and I have personally followed its advice ever since. It suggested that when you pack, you should first put everything out on your bed which you think you'll need.

Then, the article advised, you should eliminate half of it. Take a break for five minutes, and come back and cut out half of it again. Believe me, you will still have too much luggage, but you have to take a few things. Just think of a crowded airport after a ten-hour flight with no luggage trolleys available. It works every time.

Pack everything you think your children will need to feel comfortable in the hotel you may have to stay in for weeks before your new accommodation is ready. We always travel with pillow cases. We put some videotapes in the suitcase as well. Pack new toys or distractions (for yourself as well as your children) in your suitcase so you can dole them out along the way.

Have a lot of new smaller toys and books wrapped up like presents for the airplane (so your children won't discover them in the suitcase and ruin their distraction-value). Take along two of everything in case something important gets lost, like a pacifier.

Knapsacks are a good idea not only for your children's things, but for you too. If everything is on your back, it leaves your hands free to chase a child or carry something last minute.

Medical Supplies
By this point, you may be thinking I am compulsive, but I have learned a lot of lessons the hard way. When it comes to medical supplies, especially if you are headed for a Third World posting, you can never be over-prepared.

I always pack two medical kits, one for the airplane, and one for the suitcase. For on board: anti-nauseants and anti-histamines for children to help them sleep (but remember you have to experiment and pre-test baby medicine); bandages, antacid tablets for airline food (Maalox works great), eardrops just in case, eyedrops for jet lagged eyes, sleeping tablets (too optimistic but you never know and they do help you get over jet lag), baby aspirin or anything else to bring down an in-flight fever), a thermometer, throat lozenges, lip balm and extra strength adult tylenol. In the suitcase, I pack the heavier items: a rainbow assortment of cold medicines, antiseptic cleanser, Vicks vaporub, vitamins, anti-diarrhea medicine, sun screen, and topical ointments for every emergency. Anti-malarial drugs if you are heading to a destination where disease carrying mosquitos are prevalent.

SOME FINAL PRE-DEPARTURE ADVICE

Common sense is your best defense against drowning in the tidal wave of emotions and physical exhaustion which may be plaguing you at this pre-departure stage. Listen to what your own inner voice is telling you. Always remember that you do know what is best for your family and for yourself, so take the time to follow your own intuition. Moving abroad may take you onto unfamiliar ground, but motherhood doesn't recognize international borders. The instincts you have always relied upon at home need not be abandoned, just modified to reflect a change of surroundings.

Recognize your jittery mood and quick temper as being merely part of a temporary condition which does actually go away. The house will get packed up, you will actually say goodbye, you will board the airplane eventually. In fact, wait until you experience the sweet feeling of relief when you are on your way and there is nothing more to be done until you get where you're going. Savor that feeling.

It's always easier to say than do, but try not to be too hard on yourself. If your ability to be flexible momentarily disappears because you're exhausted, it will return when you've had a good night's sleep.

Give yourself a few minutes to enjoy the thought of the exotic adventure which lies ahead. And remember this: were Superwoman moving overseas, even she would have to stop and shake off a bad mood before carrying on with what works best for her.

Chapter Two

WHEN YOU ARRIVE
How to Hit the Ground Running Without Getting Your Face Smashed

"Mommy says there's no way she's ever doing this again," my seven-year-old daughter announced to her father after stepping off the Dragonair flight from Hong Kong to Beijing.

"Hi, dear," was all I could manage to mutter. My resentment and exhaustion combined to give me a kind of distorted look of despair. "We made it." Barely.

My daughter was confirming a theme I had mentioned too many times to my children during the marathon of flying we had just survived over the previous three days. ("Remember I said this," I ranted. "I'm never doing this alone again. I must have been crazy to agree to this!") My husband had headed out for Beijing two weeks ahead of his dependents. I had chosen to remain behind in Canada, esconsed at a rented cottage, absorbing and savoring a few extra weeks of Canadian summer culture. It had been marvelous and therapeutic after a stressful year in Taipei. In Canada, we could be like the party people in the beer commercials, except without the beer; the last to leave the beach; the compulsive gas barbeque users; the credit card abusers.

Arriving at Beijing's sleepy, less than upscale airport, especially after Hong Kong's frenetic Kai Tak, I was not a pretty sight. I was a woman who had just flown halfway around the world, on non-stop flights of twelve hours or more, with two young children, too much luggage, and too little mental energy to absorb yet another change in housing. To break up the journey, I had stopped in both Vancouver and Hong Kong, only to check in and out of hotels in what felt like a matter of minutes. Not unlike other traveling wives who do this every year, especially in the summer, I looked like a woman on the verge of a nervous breakdown. I was cranky and would have contemplated divorce if I didn't love my husband so much.

My children travel extraordinarily well but moments will always occur. On this particular voyage, besides the expected stresses of a long door-to-door journey, there had been a few surprises too. Halfway over the Pacific, for instance, my daughter bit into an almond forcing a gush of blood to come shooting out of her loose front tooth. Climbing over my sleeping son, I had stood on the arm rests in what could only have been perceived by fellow passengers as a hostile pose while attempting to yank the tooth from her mouth. The tooth wouldn't budge. I looked like an airborne child molester. My worldly daughter, meanwhile, wondered aloud if the tooth fairy would leave his reward in Canadian or Hong Kong dollars.

It remains my firm belief that women should not leave home without two of everything their children could possibly need along the way, including parents.

YOU MADE IT

At last, after months of taking care of the endless details of an international move (which in the real world would qualify you for a job as a Chief Executive Officer of a major corporation), you are now about to tackle the challenge of settling into a new city, a new culture, new living quarters, a new life.

The arrival period will make demands on your physical and emotional stamina which will rival your pre-departure hysteria and can sometimes push your endurance to the wall. You may not be smiling upon arrival, but there truly will be more smiles in the future. Honestly.

No matter how many times you move overseas, no matter how prepared you are to face those initial feelings of temporary limbo, regardless of Third or First World setting, the first few weeks in your new environment will be disorienting until you find you and your family's new life rhythm and routine. The good news is that like any other phase in your life, it has a beginning – and an end.

To be aware of what faces you, once you step off that airplane, will go a long way towards helping you to not only cope with the many changes in your life, but to see them as part and parcel of the overseas adventure you will one day brag about to your friends back home.

If viewed in that light, it is reassuring to know that today's trauma will be tomorrow's humorous dinner party anecdote.

Still, it can't hurt to take note of a few of the emotional hurdles you're expected to clear before the laughing part begins. So here are some of the possibilities for tears and tantrums, and I'm not just talking about your children's.

AIRPORT HASSLES

I've always felt that if a marriage has managed to survive long distance flying, then foreign airports offer one final test of mettle. During our initial trip out to Taipei (with two parents in constant attendance), I tested fate by becoming almost smug over how things had gone so well. We had flown without incident all the way through to Tokyo where we had all managed to get a little sleep (with the help of a lot of a baby anti-nauseant for our two-year-old) at a nearby hotel.

The next morning, somewhat refreshed and in high spirits, we had stuffed our faces with a hearty breakfast before catching the shuttle bus back to Narita Airport for our final flight to Taipei. The sun was shining, we were laughing with excitement, we even waved as the shuttle bus pulled away after dropping us at our terminal. Then, it hit me: the bus had made off with one of our suitcases and was already out of sight as it hustled itself back to the airport hotels for more passengers.

Naturally, I burst into hysterics (delayed reaction to sleep deprivation was my only plausible excuse). Defying the possibility of cardiac arrest, my husband took off at high speed after the bus, only to run a circle around the departure area. There were phone calls, more hysterics, flight announcements echoing around us, while my children eyed me in complete shock, wondering whether to laugh or cry. We eventually got our bags, but I wasn't too impressive that morning.

Arriving in a foreign airport offers a particular challenge, because alongside often high temperatures can come crowded, suffocating, and completely overwhelming cultural conditions. These conditions usually come in the form of a thousand screaming men all offering you a cheap taxi fare to the nearest city. And no matter the country, there will be long lineups for immigration and luggage carousels giving no indication of which flight's luggage they carry. Add to that a typical world-wide lack of luggage trolleys and ornery custom officials and you can count on feeling like you have landed – exhausted – on another planet.

For a woman who probably stepped onto her first flight in a relatively cool and crisp state of mind and apparel, such airport scenes can eat at the last of her emotional reserves, especially if her partner has come ahead and she is arriving solo, or she is weighted down by children. (This, at any rate, is my rationalization for my frazzled emotional state on arriving in Beijing.)

Whether I'm alone or with my spouse, I make sure somebody is waiting outside the customs and immigration hall to whisk us away. If you're with a company or represent your government, there will likely be an official on hand to help you through the maze. If nobody official is standing by, most airlines have representatives whose job it is to help arriving handicapped passengers. Children, in this instance, qualify you. Go with the person, regardless of their appearance.

On our first posting, an opportunity to accompany my husband on a business trip to Burma (Myanmar) came up. I decided to overlook the fact that I was seven months pregnant and likely doing the most foolish thing I'd ever done in my life. When we deplaned in Rangoon (now Yangon) from Bangkok, a journey some travel writers have described as one hour and thirty years, I was so overcome by the heat and time warp sensation brought about by the Imperial-looking airport, that I felt like fainting. Standing on the runway, enveloped by a humid fog, was our Burmese official, draped in the traditional sarong, and waving a small maple leaf at us. I thought I was delirious, but he relieved us of our passports (much to our initial dismay) and whisked us through customs in record time. Always try to make sure someone meets you at the airport.

HOTEL LIFE

It is rare that your living accommodations are ready for you instantly upon your arrival, so be prepared to camp out in a hotel for a few days, which may turn into a few weeks.

At the beginning of your assignment, a hotel room, lobby and restaurant are just institutional reminders that you're not settled properly yet. Waking up in the middle of the night in a hotel room – and then remembering where you are – can be an unhappy experience, too. I remember my own middle of the night crying jags in fluorescent-lit bathrooms all too well.

To make the hotel room easier to bear, pack as many familiar, homey items (the smaller the better) in your suitcase with you. Framed pictures of family, your child's favorite pillowcase and stuffed toy, even a photo album will go a long way to easing your feelings of homesickness. You may also miss being able to make a cup of tea or have a drink that doesn't cost an arm and a leg from the hotel refrigerator. Wherever possible and if budget permits, reserve an apartment hotel room with kitchen facilities. They are often as reasonably priced as major hotel rooms. If apartment hotels are not available, seek out the nearest supermarket and load up cheaply. Room service loses its appeal when you feel like a snack after a hot bath and aren't keen to open your door half naked to a waiter.

One word of advice if you go the apartment hotel route: check out the amenities beforehand if possible. Upon arrival at our second assignment in Taipei, we found ourselves in a half-finished apartment hotel. There was no restaurant except for an overpriced food kiosk in the unfinished lobby. Sure, we had a kitchen outfitted with a fridge and a microwave, but it had no traditional stove. Since we are about the last holdouts of microwave technology in North America, the kitchen didn't really provide us with anything we could use to feed our young children. As it was, we purchased a rice cooker immediately and served them up rice and assorted 'nuked' food for dinner at night.

Laundry can be another issue if your company is not footing the bill for the related costs of your hotel stay. Hotel laundry service is expensive, especially in cases where the cost of washing a two-year-old's T-shirt costs the same as a woman's blouse. Most hotel bathrooms come equipped with a small clothesline which helps contain the sight of drying rinsed out underwear to an out-of-the-way (and out of sight) location. Check the telephone book for the nearest laundromat if your stay is a long one and you are responsible for paying for it.

Children find it hard to camp out in hotels, despite the initial novelty. This has less to do with the rooms themselves, than with a transference of the parent's tension from being confined to small quarters and meals (always *en famille*) limited to restaurants. It's sometimes easier to say than do depending on where you're posted, but try to arrange activities special for children (errands definitely don't qualify) outside of the hotel to lessen the cabin fever which your family – and in particular you and your spouse – may be feeling.

Being trapped in a hotel room with children to entertain while your husband goes to his new office, is another emotional and physical land mine. I confess: I'm no good at all at hanging around all day with kids when I'm desperate to move into a new place and get organized.

We were put up at Beijing's Great Wall Sheraton while awaiting our move into one of the foreign compounds (I'll get to deep stress brought on by the sight of your home in a minute). Despite its five-star status, I found my blood pressure rising, pumped up by my resentment towards my husband (the one with the job) and too many room service cups of coffee. By the end of the day, awaiting his return, with no friends to share my frustration, my poor daughter had to listen to her mother's unrelenting advice: grow up to be a man if you know what's good for you.

One final word about hotel life: avoid the soaps. Hotel soap can be highly perfumed, like the bubble bath, and if you have sensitive skin, the soap will wreak havoc with your face. Three days into our hotel stay in Taipei, my face broke out in welts from the hotel soap. Imagine how much fun it was for me to be in a new city, with young children, barely over jet lag, and unable to face myself in the mirror without becoming hysterical.

SHAKING OFF JET LAG

Jet lag miracle cures are becoming almost as common now as diet books. Like weight loss programs, though, you have to have incredible self-discipline, especially if you follow the most popular jet lag cure which involves eating on alternate days or some such nonsense.

I say nonsense only because when you are moving abroad, or arriving in a strange city, the last thing you want to do is impose some strict regimen to an already overloaded emotional agenda. In my view, the extent of your jet lag will depend less on the number of time zones you move through, and more on the number of children you are traveling with and their sensitivity to the effects of baby anti-nauseants. Jet lag is no myth, it's true, so you will feel tired and your stomach will be upside down until you get used to the change of water and food. The key to a quick recovery often lies in getting at least two nights' solid sleep of eight hours in order to turn your system around.

You don't have to be as strict as the jet lag diet advocates, but do keep your eating down to a minimum. Give your stomach time to get over all the airplane food. You'll have plenty of time to sample the local fare. Tea and toast are good bland bets.

TIMING YOUR ARRIVAL

The timing of your arrival can make or break you emotionally, especially if you are traveling with school-age children. If you are moving in the summer, inquire ahead of time to discover when the school term begins. Give your children about a week to get over their jet lag and enjoy the initial honeymoon of being in a new city, but arrive no earlier. Nothing to do at home is a lot different from nothing to do overseas when you are trying to get organized and feel guilty about parking your kids in front of a video machine. Likewise, don't arrive the night before school starts and expect your children to go off willingly alone the following morning on a strange school bus. Would you, as an adult, be brave enough to venture out immediately into that great unknown?

Some expatriate communities empty out in the summer time for extended home leave. This could mean that if you arrive too early, even with the best intentions of finding new friends from the foreign community for your children or for yourself, you will come up empty. Such a situation will only fuel your family's feelings that they have left their friends behind and can't meet any new ones. Since the object upon arrival is to connect with new people, it can be disheartening to discover that there is literally no one to meet. However, you can turn these circumstances into an opportunity to befriend local folk, especially in parks or playgrounds where other mothers may be out in the morning trying to entertain little ones. Local coffee shops are another place to start up a conversation. There will naturally be language barriers in some cases, but depending on the country, you may find someone who understands you enough to get both a conversation started and a feeling on your side that you are making even the slightest contact with your new culture.

You can always act like tourists while you wait for the residents to come back. You may be exhausted from your traveling, or you may think you have lots of time to see the sights. Neither excuse is good enough; getting out and seeing your new environment will actually help combat your fatigue, which may be from sleeping too much due to boredom. Also, old hands anywhere will tell you that often you just never get around to seeing what your city is famous for, so why not start right away? It certainly is a way of getting out of the hotel, or an empty apartment awaiting its furniture. At the very least, it may reinforce some of the reasons you had for choosing your particular overseas location.

Walk, walk, walk. Soak up some local color, even if it's only a quick run outside to buy a newspaper or some aspirin. Begin familiarizing yourself with the sounds and smells you will be living with for several years. Resist any urges to be a wimp and hide away in a hotel room. The sooner you venture out alone, the sooner you will regain your own feelings of independence and self-confidence.

COMPANIES WHICH CAN HELP

We've moved overseas three times now, and our arrival experiences have all been different. The first time out, we were spoon-fed by an Embassy support system which further introduced us to an extraordinarily sensitive spouse, who to this day is my guide to what an ideal foreign service wife should be like. In fact, she was so nice, I couldn't believe she was real. On arrival at our first posting, albeit without children, we were wined, dined, introduced to both professional and personal contacts, and provided with a superb guide to the city's goods and social services – all within the first week.

The second time out in Taiwan was under slightly different circumstances and such a comprehensive support system was not part of the package. We were the first ones into a unique situation and certain perquisites and support systems were voluntarily forfeited in return for the adventure of being trailblazers. We had no emotional support, certainly not of the kind we had experienced on our first assignment overseas. I confess that I'll take the spoon-feeding any day over the indifference.

On our third time out we were partially spoon-fed. That is, we had an Embassy community to draw support from (and after Taipei, Beijing ironically seemed like paradise – everything is relative), but we nonetheless felt alienated, especially being camped out in a hotel for two very long weeks. Even with offers of help, new arrivals often don't want to risk imposing on those around them. All I can say is, go ahead and impose. The people you are feeling insecure around suffered the same feelings of isolation when they arrived and are more willing to help out than you may think.

While you can't control or select the people who will be on the other end to help you, you can control your expectations of what will be done for you. If you go out expecting a band at the airport followed by a ten-course banquet in your hotel room, you will obviously be disappointed. If you expect very little assistance in getting settled, then what you do receive will be a grateful bonus. Besides, the sooner you learn how to do things for yourself, the easier life overseas will become for you, because resourcefulness, flexibility and a good sense of humor are basic requirements to see you through those early days and the later ones, too.

Fortunately, there are professional companies or community service organizations established in most foreign cities which cater to the orientation needs of newly arrived expatriates. If you're thrown to the wolves, find one of them. In most cases, foreign embassies, international schools, even local churches will know about them.

Many of these companies offer what are known as in-country orientation programs and they will cater their services to your needs. Often, if you are allowed a 'look-see' visit before your move, it will have been coordinated by such a company. These professionals will teach you some of the basic survival skills you'll need, such as knowing where the hospitals are, and introduce you to your host culture, through lectures or articles. It is worth it to touch base with these professionals, because they can assist you not only at the beginning but throughout your stay as well by offering counseling, language training, and other adult education classes.

MEETING THE BOSS AND HIS WIFE

At this end of the moving cycle, meeting the boss and his wife can be a shakier experience. Your mind may be numb from lack of sleep, or distracted by details. You may also be quietly excusing yourself to go to the bathroom on the hour because of something you ate on the plane.

In short, it's not the greatest of times to meet someone who could have a say in your husband's career. Unfortunately, if you bow out of any meeting (and you can't do it indefinitely) it doesn't look too good either.

Instead, keep this thought in mind: the boss's wife is also a woman who probably went crazy for a while when she first arrived. She may be more sympathetic than you think. All your worries about the kind of impression you are making could just be in your head and not hers.

You are at a vulnerable stage in your life, so don't expect

miracles from yourself. If being yourself means being a distracted, sleepless, freaked out lady, that's OK too. Just try to keep it all to a minimum.

OTHER SURVIVAL TIPS FOR EARLY DAYS

About three days after settling into Beijing's Great Wall Sheraton, I felt I was ready to see the foreign diplomatic compound we were scheduled to shortly move into. At least I thought I was ready. From behind the glass windows of the hotel a dozen storeys up, life in Beijing seemed pleasant enough. Stationed on what I started calling 'Moon Station Beijing', with satellite television beaming us strange commercials from California, and room service coffee trays, I hadn't seen much at ground level. Until we took a taxi to Jianguomenwai, a run-down group of a dozen apartment blocks in which foreign diplomats and journalists are kept a safe distance from the Chinese.

I went into deep culture shock. My brain froze, refusing to accept this new reality, especially after the sight of our own building and the bars surrounding our ground floor apartment. I simply wasn't ready for the sight of what – to me anyway – looked like a low-income housing unit. Spying the filthy, garbage laden entrance way to our own apartment did not make matters better. Cruising by the 'playground', littered with old equipment from McDonald's, which also gave the playground its name, I started to picture every kind of disaster which could befall my children.

My negative attitude towards the playground only got worse after one Jianguomenwai dweller laughingly told me about an incident in the playground: two African children got into a fight, and when their diplomat fathers came out to settle the matter, one killed the other. Who knew if the story was true? I wanted to run away, and did. From the experience of friends, I am able to picture other, equally demoralizing scenarios vividly. You have finally left the hotel and moved into your home for the next few years. (Beijing's foreign compound is an exception, not the rule.) Even if it's furnished, there will still be your own knickknacks to arrive and pictures for the empty walls.

If you're in the Third World, there may be servants standing by to do your every bidding, including your cooking, shopping, cleaning, and baby-sitting. If there are no children to get organized, or they are already off to school, you are sitting on your brand new couch, watching the servants watch you. It is only 7 a.m. and your spouse has already left for work. You wonder what to do next. Here are some ideas.

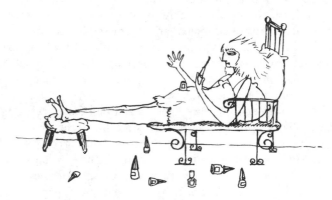

Do Something Nice For Yourself
I'm not into manicures or beauty treatments in general, but under certain circumstances they represent the ideal pampering tool. Go for it. Or go for anything which makes you happy: a new piece of clothing, an hour by yourself away from the family, a piece of chocolate cake in the hotel lobby or nearest bakery.

Another suggestion, and I am not being trite: never overlook the importance of trashy novels during this post-arrival period. You likely never had a chance to read before you left home, and the airplane may have had other distractions (like the need to constantly entertain children) so now that you have a little time on your hands which can't be filled with anything too useful, sit back and read a book. Don't read all those heavy reference books on your new country at this point (unless they are about goods and services, and clubs). Escape into a trashy novel. Just don't spend all of your time in fictional never never land. You can't blot out your environment forever.

Get On the Phone and the Internet

Use the phone as much as you can and pray you're in a country where the phone works well enough not to set off an adult-sized temper tantrum. If you've been given the names of people beforehand, call them up and arrange to get together.

The Internet, often accused of isolating people, has in fact been a wonderful point of connection for expats so try to get your computer hooked up as quickly as possible in order to get on line. Obviously, e-mail can never replace face to face conversations but in the early days, it will be one way to feel less isolated from family and friends. More and more expatriate communities are also setting up web sites to help newcomers find things in their new cities. Find out if there is one where you are living and log on. It is also nice to keep in touch with news from back home so check to see if your hometown paper, even your favorite magazine, has on on-line version you can read or print out.

Avoid Temptation

Spouses without children often find the late afternoons the hardest part of the day to deal with, especially at the beginning when you have few friends to call up for a chat.

The daytime hours can be filled with long walks and errands, but dusk provides a new challenge because there could be several hours when you are awaiting the return of your spouse from work. Some women confess they find themselves having a glass of wine to pass the time, and quickly find they are having several glasses before they know it. It's best to leave an activity – a walk around the block, letter writing, or a swim – for those end-of-the-day hours.

Day Trips

Depending on your spouse's work, the early days can often offer familiarization trips outside the city, to a factory, a branch office, a refugee camp, or hospital.

Wherever possible, arrange to go along on those trips so that you can also familiarize yourself with your host country and some of the problems it may be facing. It is refreshing to get an outside perspective and discover that the country itself may be far different from its capital city. You may also get to meet some of your husband's new colleagues which will help when he starts talking about them. You will be able to put faces to names.

Start Your Photo Album

Amateur photographers who move abroad will tell you: take all your pictures within the first six months of your arrival in a new country. That is the time when things still look fresh to you. Often after you've lived somewhere a while, you start to overlook the sights which startled you in the beginning. If you plan to make a visual record of your stay, begin as soon as possible. It is a good project for the early days. The same can be said for journal writing. While you may continue to jot down memories later on, write when your observations are at their freshest.

YOU HAVEN'T INVENTED RESENTMENT

A journal is a benign outlet for the feelings of frustration and resentment you may be feeling towards your spouse. At least the paper can't get into an argument with you. I've met a lot of 'accompanying' spouses and haven't yet found one who didn't at one time or another feel overwhelming resentment towards their spouses for bringing them to some 'godforsaken place!'

In the early days, it's also not unusual to go around screaming "It's your fault!" at your spouse, blaming him for everything from a stained blouse, to a bad haircut, and of course, the fact that you feel overweight and out of shape. Resentment is usually at its most intense soon after you arrive. For one thing, after the traveling is over, and all the adrenalin which kept you going through the preparations stops pumping, your emotions tend to come crashing down in the worst way. These are also the days when you are at your most vulnerable. You've left your friends and family behind, your environment is still strange and unfriendly, and you are in a waiting period until your new life has taken shape.

If you are a naturally independent person, you may resent the feelings of dependence you have on your spouse, for money, for entertainment, even for his help in making a doctor's appointment. If you're a career person who has put your's on hold, there will be further resentment.

If someone can come up with a sure-fire method of avoiding these feelings, they could make a million dollars patenting it. Until then, the only way around it is to recognize those particular reasons which fuel resentment and then work out a strategy for avoiding them. From experience, I've identified three factors (and some coping mechanisms) which often encourage resentment at the beginning of your posting.

(1) Isolation

After culture shock (which I will deal with later in chapter three) I place feelings of isolation highest on my list of emotions which feed my antagonism towards my husband. I blame him for taking me away from everything which is familiar, comforting, easy to handle, and capable of making me act like a normal person instead of a manic depressive with wild mood swings. When I am isolated (by myself, feeling sorry for myself) I am no good to anyone.

Arguments are pointless because after all, we are here to stay so what is the use of saying everything is better back home? The only solution is to end the isolation by making my new environment familiar, comforting, easy to handle, and turning myself back into a normal person with only occasional mood swings (I never said I was perfect). As much as it may frighten me, I make the effort to learn about my new environment by getting into a taxi or going for long walks where I make countless discoveries like: there's the post office, there's where I can rent a video, there's the bookstore, they do sell my favorite makeup here, there is a fabulous curio shop where I can browse forever, etc.

Returning from those walks, I will invariably bring something back home which makes our apartment or house friendlier, more inviting, like colorful fans for the walls, baskets for plants, pillows. You don't need a lot of money for these little outings, but make sure you bring your confidence, especially if you're posted to a place like Bangkok where the taxis have no meters and you have to bargain for a fare.

To make my life easier to handle, I also establish a routine such as it may be, like nap with my son: 12–1. Work at gaining control over some part of your day and let the rest fall into place. To make friends, each person has to come up with their own strategy which fits their personality, but as a general rule overseas, learn to make the first move and introduce yourself. Find a common point of interest and make a date to get together. Don't just say it either: pull out your date book and set a day on the spot. Isolation quickly ends when people come into your life.

(2) Money

A fly on the wall of an overseas household could tell great tales about arguments over money and how all those overseas benefits should be spent. A more common sore point can be the resentment a spouse may feel if they are given an allowance when they live away. This can happen if banking is difficult or inaccessible. Many women prefer to keep some personal channels of banking open to avoid what can be tight financial control overseas by their husbands. Since both my husband and I have always kept our budget controlled by allowances, I have never minded them, but have always used credit cards as an escape valve.

On our posting in Taiwan, I faced a cash-only society and had to think fast before I got too depressed. We found a solution that could work for others: have money assigned only for your use that is completely outside of that you use for the necessities of life. Call it what you like – pin money, fun money – just make sure it's up to you how it is spent. The important thing is to reach an agreement with your partner so the money issue doesn't become a major source of resentment between you.

(3) Career

Except for couples who go overseas to work as husband and wife teams such as foreign aid workers, World Health Organization medical officers, missionaries and some teachers, most of the time, 'accompanying' wives with careers back home would have given them up in order to follow their husbands abroad. If you've put your career on hold to travel, you could now be resenting the hell out of your spouse for it.

For some reason, the reality of such decisions never really hits home until you are in your new home and have no office to go to or deadline to meet. It sounded great telling your friends before you left that you were going to look for something new, or take a sabbatical, but once you are overseas, you find you are devastated the first time someone asks you what you do and you're tongue-tied for a response.

The bad news is that you will probably never get over giving up a career so either get used to it or find something to work at. The good news is, nobody will likely ask you what you do. I'm not being cynical about this, just truthful. In overseas settings, especially the Third World where working is hassled and benefits high enough so that a spouse isn't forced to find a second income, women are rarely asked if they are working, have worked, hope to work, etc. That's not to say you won't meet local working women and be envious of their situations, but working spouses overseas are the exception rather than the rule. This means your feelings of resentment will not be sparked too often by outsiders, but will mostly be your own demon to deal with.

DON'T BE SO HARD ON YOURSELF

There can be no perfect score in clearing all the emotional hurdles which will lie in your path when you move abroad, so go easy on yourself. Just as I advised you to have as few expectations as you can of the welcome you will receive, by the same token, give yourself a break and temper your expectations of yourself, your spouse, and your children.

Especially at the beginning, you and your family are under a great deal of stress. Perfect behavior, whether it be table manners or sensitivity, just can't always be delivered. Likewise, don't get upset over your weight, your hair, your clothes and all of those other emotional land mines which can make your life miserable if they blow up on you. (I felt a face rash merited some self-pity but I managed to get past it with the help of a lot of will power and strict avoidance of mirrors.)

Your environment may also not live up to your expectations if you set them too high. Your new home will not be like the home and country you left, so the sooner you start accepting the changes in the way you live, the better off you will be. Learn to substitute local products for the ones you preferred at home; find new areas of interest and friends to replace the ones left behind; stop yourself from making constant comparisons between old and new; schools, housing, everything in fact which could ruin your new life for you.

You have moved physically, and the sooner you move mentally, too, the better you will feel. It is completely counterproductive, to say nothing of a waste of a good overseas posting, to spend all your time recreating your old environment.

YOU WILL GET SETTLED EVENTUALLY

It won't happen overnight, but gradually street corners, shops, even traffic will become familiar to you and 'back home' will become thoughts you will take out and enjoy occasionally like a family photo album. The phone will start ringing, your date book will have notations in it that are not just lists of things to get done, and you'll find yourself out for an evening with good friends you suddenly realize you have known for less than two months.

You may not believe it, but it will happen. Your shipment will arrive, your home will assume a more cluttered air, your children will be out with friends, you may even get used to hot, spicy food or plain boiled food, depending on which part of the world you're in. The arrival period which seemed so endless, like all those flights it took you to get there, will be over so that finally you can get on with the adventure of life abroad.

— Chapter Three —

MAKING THE CULTURAL TRANSITION
Having the Sh*t Scared Out of You

I once wrote the script for a briefing video for foreign aid workers going overseas. I eventually titled the program 'Culture Shocked!' Its purpose was straightforward enough – to help ease the problems of cultural transition.

Before actually writing the opening sequence, I forced my mind to drift back to our first posting to Thailand. I wanted to retrieve my memories of my own first experience with extreme culture shock. Though it had been years earlier, I was still able to conjure up a clear picture of the precise moment I stepped out of the airplane into a humid inferno that is the all season temperature of Bangkok. I had paused momentarily at the top of a portable staircase, and gazed blindly into the blazing, cloudless sky. Uneasy on my feet, I had slowly and carefully negotiated the staircase. When I reached the bottom, with barely a moment to attempt a deep breath, I was briskly shoved from behind into the airport shuttle bus which seemed to have neither front nor back, just a packed core full of menacing-looking people.

I was sure I had screamed *help!*, but my husband had just smiled reassuringly at me without speaking. But my head felt like it was about to lose the blood which sustained it. My throat dried up. There was sweat running down my back (could backs sweat like that? I remember wondering) and I frantically gripped my husband's arm while we were transported barely a few hundred yards.

When the doors opened again, passengers who had sat politely on the airplane for several hours, were suddenly energized enough to rush down steamy colorless corridors to ensure they were the first to be processed through an immigration lineup I was positive stretched back to the tarmac. Though we hadn't even entered the main terminal yet, I knew I was going to vomit all over my hand luggage because my head and stomach were doing somersaults. I barely made it to an airport cleaner's closet before heaving my shock into a pail.

But first impressions, even vivid ones like mine, aren't the entire story of culture shock. I knew if I were to write a twenty-minute film on the subject which would be useful, I still needed to fill in the gaps in my knowledge. I was directed to a specialist in culture shock to help me with my research. This professional – a well-worn traveler himself – was known as an 'animator' in the briefing business.

Afterwards, I remember thinking the title suited him well, for in the most animated of states, he responded to my opening question – "What is culture shock anyway?" – with a truly succinct reply which captured the crux of the issue.

"Culture shock," he said, "is when you have the shit scared out of you."

I hesitated for a minute, slightly nonplussed. Then, I

remembered my own arrival in Bangkok, and my subsequent love affair with the toilet in the early days of our assignment.

"You mean...like diarrhea?" I asked.

"I mean exactly that," he responded before suggesting we name the film along this theme in the interests of accuracy.

A HUMAN EARTHQUAKE

He was right, if not slightly graphic. One of the first signs of cultural disorientation can be a revolt of your insides, from both ends. You will struggle to remember what you've eaten (was it the airplane food?), what you may have had to drink with bad ice in it, or perhaps you'll blame malarial tablets or anything else new which you've ingested along the way. Any or all of those things may be the culprit, but do not overlook the strong physical shock waves – a response to the over-stimulation of your new surroundings – washing over you that can affect your body as well as your mind. You are being bombarded with strange new images, often in sub-zero weather or sweltering heat, with a cacophony of noise swirling around your head. The smells alone of a strange city can do a number on your tummy.

Three days after our arrival in Beijing, my husband decided it was time I saw Jianguomenwai, the biggest of the foreign compounds where diplomats and journalists are segregated into a modern-day Forbidden City. Like the days of the reigning emperors, ordinary Chinese people are kept out of this mini-city of apartment blocks unless they have the appropriate paper to allow them entry to work, not visit.

I thought I was ready to see the apartment building I would live in for the next two years. After all, I had just spent a year in Taiwan, and I was no neophyte to the Third World. Our taxi dropped us off near the McDonald's playground I mentioned earlier (the one I instantly assessed as being too unsafe for my children to play in) and I could feel my brain descending simultaneously into both deep stress and deep culture shock. The littered entranceway to our apartment building (we didn't even have a key to go into the apartment but had to settle for a glimpse of a dark, dreary entranceway) only made matters worse. I had to get out of there. But where did we go? To the nearby Friendship Store, where the sights and smells provided the final blow to my shakey emotional state. Back to the hotel! Now!

In a similar vein, many accompanying wives of students from the tropics, studying in Western countries, have recalled their initial horror at seeing the damp and dingy married students' quarters which they've had to pay unreasonably high rent for. A few confessed that it made their skin literally creep to see the moss growing on the walls of their kitchens and bathrooms.

I met an Egyptian woman once who confided that while her culture shock to Canada was pretty limited after growing up surrounded by foreigners in the cosmopolitan city of Alexandria, she will never forget the surprise she felt when the temperature plummeted to minus forty in Winnipeg, the first Canadian city she and her husband lived in. The surprise was the discovery that she actually preferred cold weather to hot, although minus forty degrees was a bit extreme.

In another instance of culture shock, a Taiwanese friend, married to a Canadian foreign service officer, said the shock of arriving in clean, orderly Canada was compounded further by the fact that rules – of the road especially – were actually followed by law-abiding Canadians. Speaking of roads, even driving on different sides of the road can be so disorientating as to lead to headache and nausea.

Certain social customs of the 'host' country can often lead to bewilderment too. For example, in England, where handling the produce at the greengrocer's is practically taboo, many African, Asian and Latin American wives have had the wrath of irate greengrocers descend upon them. Unaware of the custom, and used to selecting their own purchases at market stalls in their own countries, they had innocently touched the delicate tomatoes and other vegetables during their first 'solo' attempts at shopping for food. Such abrupt 'initiation rites' definitely do not relieve the angst of rookie expatriate wives. With similar strange – to you at least – scenes and attitudes swirling around you, it's no wonder you feel overwhelmed and giddy when you first arrive in a new city. You have fallen into a kind of phantom zone. A reality still exists out there but you are seeing a different view of it.

Culture shock is an individual's first reaction to an uncertain and different environment. 'Culture' is the new way of life to which you are being exposed; 'shock' is your physical and emotional response to that different way of living. In every country of the world, people share a particular view about living. When you move to a new country, that view is different, often radically, from the view you are used to. A neophyte traveler often makes the mistake of believing that another country's view of life is the wrong view. Nothing could be further from the truth. In matters of culture, there is no right or wrong – only different. Keep that uppermost in your mind, and your tenure abroad will be a lot more satisfying and rewarding. Remember the Ugly American? Try to avoid becoming the Ugly Expatriate.

EVERYBODY SUFFERS CULTURE SHOCK

Not even a seasoned traveler can step off an airplane in a strange city and make an immediate adjustment. When you're a tourist, you are paying good money to experience exotic adventure and a change from the humdrum everyday life back home. But when you arrive in a foreign country and know you'll be staying for a few years, the culture shock can be much more frightening and certainly will have a wider scope. You can't just brush it off with the knowledge that it will all be over in a few weeks. You will have to live with the different smells, climate, language, traffic conditions, poor people, too rich people (that can shock you, too, believe me) or any other signs of cultural differences which strike you upon arrival.

YOU CAN CHART THE STAGES

Culture shock has a life cycle of its own, usually lasting about six months. There are also very distinct stages, so be prepared by knowing how to identify them:

Tourist/Honeymoon Stage

This is the easiest of all the stages to spot. You've just arrived. You may have been overwhelmed at the airport for a few minutes, but that was the jet lag. Now everything looks charming. The hotel you're staying at provides a protective cocoon. They speak English and want to assist you. Everything requires a photo and talking to people on the street is fun even if they are scaring your fair-haired children to death by pinching their cheeks or stroking their hair. You jump into the new culture, eating everything in sight. Often you need the security of another person showing you around, but generally you're open to it all. The day-to-day hardships haven't set in yet.

This stage usually lasts until you've been in your new house or apartment a few weeks. If you have a two-year-old in tow, as we did our second time out, you usually skip this stage and go straight to the crisis stage which is next.

Crisis Stage

The novelty wears off. The phone won't work. All those people showing you around at the beginning have resumed their own lives and expect you to get on with yours. Your frustration levels rise as you try to put your house in order, sign your kids up for activities. You've spent an entire day trying to buy something you forgot in your shipment. Things don't work and you can't explain to anyone what you need done. You feel like a child yourself, learning to speak again. If you find yourself lashing out in anger every few minutes, especially at your husband, you know you've hit the crisis stage.

Flight Stage

So what do you want to do with all this hostility? Pack it up and head for the airport. Running away seems like a viable option, if not physically on a 747, then mentally into a novel which you read all day. You may try to forget entirely that you're overseas by immersing yourself in all those videotapes you brought along. The last thing you want to do is go out and do things, or meet new people, even if that's ultimately the key to getting over your culture shock.

Period of Readjustment

Relax! It's the end of the culture shock cycle. It's a condition which goes away like a bad cold. You do somehow emerge at the other end of the tunnel, even if the ride has been bumpy or made you ill along the way.

You manage to chill out and life resumes a pattern similar to what you had at home, albeit with a different backdrop. You wake up, you plan your day, you live your life as best you can, and you remind yourself that one day in the future you will be able to tell great stories at a dinner party about the horrible culture shock you went through. Or write a book about it.

WHY DID I COME?

Depression, acute unhappiness, resentment, fear, loss of identity and privacy, longing for your own wonderful support system back home, and let's not forget crying, crying, crying. These are also the hallmark emotions of the onset of a wife's culture shock. In other words, you are scared out of your wits about your new life, but are desperately trying not to show it. Panic is written all over your face. Or you think it is, which is just as bad. You sit in a chair, staring off into space, chanting a dazed mantra: "Why the hell did I come here? Why the hell did I come here?"

Your husband – the reason you are in this situation – comes home from work and you jump all over him for reasons which you know sound foolish even as you're saying them. For example, "The maid put the cutlery in the wrong drawer"; or, my favorite: "I took the kids to McDonald's and it was awful! There were no napkins, your son spilled his milk and nobody helped with the stroller."

None of these are truly life threatening situations but they are exactly the kind of scenarios which throw you off balance. The larger issues in life you can handle; it's the minor details which irritate you out of your mind and make you think you want to go home. You haven't even come close to understanding the host culture yet, but you know you hate it and want to leave it. Hello, culture shock.

THE ABSENT HUSBAND

Life could be worse. Think of the women who have to handle all this trauma on their own, and there are many. I've been lucky enough to never have to deal with this one, but some wives watch their husbands go out the door for a week long trip only moments after they've arrived in the new country, leaving their wives to open bank accounts, stock the cupboards, and settle the children into school.

Naturally, such trips can't be postponed (a likely story) and so many women are suddenly thrust not only in a new place, but are left to deal with it entirely on their own. If that happens to you, make a friend as quickly as possible, perhaps a seasoned expatriate wife with a sympathetic face or a local neighbor to help you with the language barrier.

AN APPEARANCE OF SUDDEN WEALTH/POVERTY

Depending on where you are living, that is, Third or First World country, another influence on your culture shock could be the sudden change in your standard of living from what you were accustomed to at home. Cars and drivers, maids, gardeners, luxurious houses or apartments are suddenly your new way of life; alternatively, laundromats, bicycle repair shops and Do-It-Yourself stores could become your usual hangouts. You feel disoriented because you truly are living in a new world, both inside and outside your home.

When we were living in Bangkok, the *Jewel in the Crown* mini-series was opening people's eyes to the lifestyles of the Raj colonial families. I had borrowed copies of the series from the local video shop, and was watching an episode one day with another friend also assigned to Bangkok.

We were both remarking on the good life of the Raj during a scene in which Indian bearers were circulating a party with cocktails for the memsahibs and sahibs. No sooner had we finished criticizing the laziness of those old India hands, when my Thai maid knocked discreetly at the door. "Madame, I have your lunch," she said, entering with a tray laden with neatly laid out sandwiches and a pot of coffee. Whoops.

AND WHAT ABOUT THE CHILDREN?

A week after we arrived in Taipei on our second posting, my then six-year-old daughter, an extremely well-adjusted mature child (I'm sure I'll pay for that when she's a teenager) suddenly burst into tears for no apparent reason. Her younger brother hadn't thrown anything at her; she wasn't coming down with something; she appeared normal if maybe just a little pale in the face. She had seemed to be enjoying the move so far, and I wondered what might have brought on the tears.

"I miss my friends!" she finally articulated to me after much coaxing.

"I miss my friends, too!" I answered her, before going back to my motherly role and comforting this sad little girl.

I thought about that particular day's events for a clue to what may have triggered her distress. We had, in fact, that very day had a brief orientation with a professional support organization. My children had been left for several hours with a baby-sitter so that my husband and I could gather the information we needed without distraction. It was the first time she had been separated from us – even briefly – in the entire three-week period we had been on the road traveling and resettling.

KIDS HAVE CULTURE SHOCK, TOO

My daughter was suffering from kiddie culture shock. Once I had made my diagnosis, I could see that both my daughter and my toddler son were experiencing similar symptoms of the adult version, if slightly modified for youthful concerns. My daughter had passed out of the honeymoon stage, momentarily, and reached her first 'crisis,' precipitated by a separation, not unlike the first time I had ventured out alone into the strange streets of a new city. She was feeling unsure of herself. Insecure without a parent there to stabilize her, hence the tears and fears.

My toddler – a two-year-old at that time – experienced culture shock in a much more vocal way. A temper tantrum which continued for two months seemed to be his reaction to his new environment. I could hardly blame the little guy. In Canada we had been living in a rural environment where he saw maybe a dozen people a week, and suddenly he was in Taiwan where even in an elevator, there would be a dozen people sharing it with us, all poking and prodding him to death because of his blonde hair.

Many children regress in reaction to the new culture. A toilet-trained toddler may suddenly wet his pants; a ten-year-old boy may suddenly need a stuffed animal to sleep with again; a fifteen-year-old girl suddenly wants to read in her room and not go out her bedroom door.

SEASONAL CULTURE SHOCK

Just when you think your children have adjusted to their new home, along comes a holiday which plunges them back into a depression. During our first Christmas in Taipei, I couldn't understand why my otherwise happy daughter seemed so down and listless. Granted, her best chum in our block had taken off for Hawaii for two weeks, but I kept feeling something else was on my daughter's mind. This was more than sheer excitement over the pending holiday. Finally I dragged it out of her. Christmas, she said, just didn't feel right without snow. And why couldn't we have a real tree instead of that fake job from Toys-R-Us lighting up our living room? It just wasn't the same. She wanted to be home for Christmas.

Making the cultural transition for children, not unlike their parents, is a year round proposition, at least for the first year overseas. Watch for mood changes at holidays, birthdays, or other annual milestones which may make your children long for the way such occasions were marked at home.

MORE WAYS TO HELP YOUR CHILDREN

Patience is indeed a virtue, and never will it be the virtue it becomes overseas. Good luck! At the very least, do the best you can, especially if you have a toddler with you.

Thoughtful gestures work well, too. Here are a few other tried and true methods of dealing with kiddie culture shock:

(1) Recognize the Signs

A temper tantrum or soiled panties are the easy clues. Mood swings, unexplained tears, lack of appetite and sleeplessness are also obvious signs. Less noticeable are the social ones which may happen while your children are at school. Discipline problems, inattention to homework or the inability to make new friends because the old ones were nicer, are all definite symptoms of a child's culture shock.

Some children, like adults, become more accident prone, or seem to be sick with flu or colds more often. Normally gregarious children who suddenly become sullen are also having problems of adaptation.

(2) Routines Can Save the Day

It may be difficult while settling in, but the sooner you establish a new routine for your culture shocked child, the better off he or she will be. The security of a schedule – bedtime especially – will help put your child back on track. School age children are in the best position to get over this transition period because a day at school provides a timetable and fixed activities.

A toddler is more problematic (I know this from experience) but even my toddler son finally leveled out a few weeks after settling into a morning nursery school program. Weekends should also be structured as much as possible.

(3) Familiar Foods and Other Signs of Home

Once your shipment from home arrives, with toys and other familiar knickknacks, life gets better for your children. While you can't recreate home, and wouldn't want to or the point of moving abroad would be lost entirely, it helps to reassure your children that life may have changed, but not completely. Food especially helps. It is possible in most countries to find food which approximates what my daughter calls 'normal' food – that is, anything they were used to eating at home whether it be Cheerios, Kraft dinner or plain white rice. Sure you'd like them to eat other kinds of food, but don't offer it every day. Alternate ethnic food with their food of choice.

(4) Communicating is More Important Than Ever

It's often easy to let your children's concerns get lost in the shuffle of organizing your new life, but now more than ever it becomes critical to really listen to what your children are telling you. Indulge their whims a bit more than you may at home, at least in the beginning.

I'm not advocating we turn our expatriate children into spoiled brats (which is an easy pitfall) but their smaller fancies should be followed up, like the way they want to decorate their bedrooms, or their request for friends to visit even if it's not terribly convenient for you. New friendships will help your child adjust faster than anything else, so don't throw cold water on after-school play dates.

In the first weeks, it may be necessary to knock on doors around you in order to help your child connect with new friends. Be prepared to do that, or to cold-call mothers on a class list to see if they are interested in getting the children together.

(5) Teach Them a Few Words of the New Language

Your children may not need as much fluency in the local tongue as you will, but it doesn't hurt to try to teach them a few words so they can communicate a bit when they are settling in. Being a linguist of questionable ability myself, I found my daughter teaching me more than I could teach her. But teaching them the basic 'please' and 'thank you' right away could help them feel less alienated from their new culture. If your children attend a local school, as do some children of missionaries and visiting scholars, it won't be long before they'll be teaching you whole sentences *and* correcting your accent as well.

(6) Parent-Child Relationships

Whatever your relationship before you left home, be prepared to restructure it when you move abroad. To say you are now needed – when the idea wouldn't cross your child's head at home – is an understatement. Parents are the constant, the symbol of stability and continuity, in an otherwise changing world. As a mother, you are thrust once again into an extreme nurturing situation, regardless of age.

When your teenager tells you that you've ruined her life by taking her away from her friends, you have to be patient and explain that while that may be true, such ruination is only short-term, like the duration of culture shock. When your toddler son embarks on an endless temper tantrum (and you secretly envy him for the fact that he can run around the room in circles crying, because you want to do the same) you have to recognize that what worked at home for discipline and general mothering, may need to be modified overseas. Patience and a sense of humor are definitely the order of the day – and some days it will seem a very tall order to fill.

(7) The Parents' Dynamics Affect the Children

If the parents are barely on speaking terms after two weeks in a hotel, no quality time together, and the endless paperwork and legwork in establishing a new household, imagine how that tension affects an uncertain and insecure child who has just been dragged to what seems like the ends of the earth. The most difficult task of all in helping your child cope with culture shock, can be trying to act happy around your children when the anxiety is mounting with each passing moment.

Likewise, taking out your adult frustration by shouting at your children just because they did something like jump on a hotel bed because they have absolutely no place to run, is hardly going to make a child feel like he's ever going to adapt to his new environment. Make sure mommy and daddy aren't as different in their behavior as the street outside.

A CHECKLIST TO DEAL WITH YOUR OWN SHOCK

If you are going to get through it – and I can't stress enough that culture shock isn't terminal – it helps to keep this survival checklist nearby for constant reference. It may not stop the tears, but it could help you get on with your new life overseas once the tears stop.

Participation is the Key

The only way to become part of your new environment is to jump right into it and become an active participant. This doesn't have to happen the very next day after you arrive, but small steps can be taken at first, like reading the local papers to get a handle on the country's issues, or expatriate magazines and newsletters to see what the foreign community is all about. Later, after the dust has settled and your children are in school, you can seek out activities for yourself, whether that may be a language course (a great way to meet other newcomers) or other life courses offered around town.

Club memberships, the YWCA if there is one, support groups, or helping out with your children's activities are other ways of joining in the local action. Talk with people you meet to find out how they keep busy. Volunteer work may be easy to find, and serve the dual purpose of helping yourself and others.

Seek Support

Local community services centers have sprung up in many foreign communities around the world, offering courses on the host culture in addition to solid orientation advice and counseling services.

Do not be afraid to ask those professionals to assist you in your transition period. Ad hoc support groups, for young mothers or people with common problems, also abound and should be checked out. Consider those groups even if you have never belonged to one in your life. An international mothers' group in Bangkok – which helped organize playgroups or just provide the latest information on the availability of Pampers – practically saved my life, in addition to introducing me to some of the finest women I know. In cities like Beijing where there are no professional organizations, start your own support group. Three other women – less even – is all it takes.

Establish New Support Systems

Feelings of isolation can be intense when you are far away from friends and family, so it is critical that you find new substitutes early on. This can be as simple as establishing one solid friendship with another woman you feel you can phone every day just to shoot the breeze or compare reactions to the new culture. Having someone you feel you can call in an emergency – especially if your husband travels a lot at the beginning – can ease a lot of your culture shock related stress. Support systems may also include items like a good VCR to entertain your children, baby-sitters, a reliable local grocer or seamstress. Think of all the people who helped you function back home, and then assemble a new set of support "staff."

Appreciate Cultural Differences

You've moved to a new culture so don't shut it out. Neither should you make judgments based on five minutes of research. Remember that many of the cultures you may be dismissing out of hand have been around a lot longer than yours and deserve more than a cursory examination before deciding they're no good. Everyone has a different way of doing things, even back home within your own neighborhood, so consider cultural differences as something positive rather than negative, worth learning and caring about to strengthen your own character and values.

Many Adjustments May Have Been
Necessary at Home

On our first posting, we had our first child and our lives were thrown into the chaos only a baby brings to the home. While Bangkok likely exaggerated certain new restrictions in our lives, we would have had the same ones at home (and certainly not the inexpensive help). Don't blame a bad marriage or a sour child-parent relationship on your new environment. Sometimes the new city may not help matters, but problems and adjustments were just as likely to have cropped up at home.

IT'S NOT JUST THE FOREIGN CULTURE THAT WILL SHOCK YOU

I was a guest at a dinner party near the beginning of our second posting abroad, when I sensed something was missing from the conversation around our table. While the women were politely drawing out their male dinner companions on the subject of their careers, their past lives, and their general philosophy towards life and the host culture, the courtesy was not being reciprocated. So I tried to interject with a few references to my own career, past life, and general philosophy.

"I'm actually a journalist by training," I began tentatively, hoping that someone would care.

"So how's business for you?" one of the men inquired of the other, before I realized the cue had not only been ignored, it had been left to dry in the wind.

I decided to return to my fork and knife, and angle for another entry point.

"You know," I tried again over dessert, "I've done a lot of work in corporate communications. I imagine there's a lot of pro-active marketing of Taiwan going on around here." There, I thought, some power speak.

"That's nice," one man commented. "My wife weaves."

THE GREAT LEAP BACKWARD

You think I'm kidding. Sad to say, I'm not. In many foreign communities overseas, a woman's feeling of disorientation, a key factor in culture shock, is often just as much a result of a time warp back to the days of the 'little woman,' as it is from tasting hot food and living with a billion people. It can be a double dose of culture shock – a reaction to the unfamiliarity of the foreign culture, and alienation from your own as well.

I don't want to take anything away from the men assigned

overseas who have no choice but to work long hours, because sometimes they just can't help but leave their wives with the bulk of the responsibilities concerning the family. There's often little choice for them.

Likewise, I've seen firsthand the life of a busy diplomat who must wine and dine for his country at endless banquets or receptions, or travel with visiting widget salesmen or government ministers.

The question is: How do those men act once they come home? Do they instantly try to balance the equation? Or do they tell their wives they're too tired to go out and the wife is being selfish for asking, even if she hasn't been outside of her home for a week?

Herein lies the separation between a loving husband and father, and a SOB who has decided everything will be his way or no way during your overseas assignment. By the way, this latter personality type usually produces the ill-bred chaps who don't bother to ask a woman seated next to him at a dinner table if she ever had a professional life – just even an original thought – before moving abroad with her husband.

WHERE IS GLORIA STEINEM WHEN YOU NEED HER?

To cope with this male chauvinism abroad, you are certainly not expected to transform yourself into Donna Reed or Beaver Cleaver's mother overnight regardless of the dominant male attitudes. But as I haven't found a guide book yet which even acknowledges – never mind prepares women – for this social regression endemic to expatriate culture, I think it's important to finally raise the issue in order that coping mechanisms, and not artificial ones, can be found.

Where does this male chauvinism spring from? Voluntary withdrawal from the work force, often because spousal employment can be downright inconvenient and hassled, and generous overseas allowances, both contribute to a resumption of fifties style one-income marriages. They can also encourage a return to perceived prerogatives some men assume are automatically assigned to the Major Breadwinner such as golfing all weekend, or staying out late at night entertaining clients.

I've seen evidence and heard firsthand testimony which supports the idea that this Retro Macho Man may have been the most liberated of chaps at home. But once he hits the overseas life, the rules of equality vanish, usually with words like: "You have servants. What more do you want?"

SO WHICH SHOCK SHOULD YOU DEAL WITH FIRST?

Adjusting to the foreign culture is definitely your first priority, since it may take a few weeks before the aftershocks from the new social conditions sink in.

Also, the shock of your own culture overseas – like male chauvinism – can be dealt with a lot more effectively after you're used to the host culture and your self-confidence has returned to previous levels. There's no point arguing a position until your feet are firmly planted on your new ground. Understand the basic stages of foreign culture shock before tackling this corollary issue – the battle of the sexes – which may develop in your own home.

And don't step out of your door without your sense of humor. If you can't laugh at it all, and at yourself for throwing temper tantrums over the most ridiculous of things, there's no point in leaving home.

— Chapter Four —

Now What?

How a Spouse Can Avoid 'Nothing to Do' Syndrome

"...The first sign of deterioration is when a woman omits her corsets from her toilette, and begins lolling about in a sloppy and tumbled tea-gown."

—from *BELOW THE PEACOCK FAN: First Ladies of the Raj,* by Marian Fowler

I'm hardly memsahib material, and I've never owned a tea-gown, but I can still vividly recall lolling about a New York apartment hotel room in sloppy jeans and a tumbled T-shirt, while my husband strutted out the door in a new pin-stripe three-piece suit, optimistically beginning his diplomatic career at the United Nations.

After the door had slammed on Mr. Future Ambassador, I remember trying hard to rechannel my resentment energy into something constructive. But I could only unpack our suitcases for so long since we had traveled light for a mere three-month assignment at the General Assembly. And I didn't care to rearrange the hotel's furniture or decorate its bland institutional decor.

I did tackle something useful, stocking up the fridge, but ended up experiencing New York-style culture shock when I innocently wandered into a nearby grocery store and was robbed, not by a mugger, but by the owner's inflated idea of what can legally be charged for a lamb chop in midtown Manhattan.

Situated where I was – equidistant between Bloomingdales and Saks – it should have been a dream come true, for I was a newly-married woman at the time, without children. And as a longstanding student of the Arts and Leisure section of the *Sunday New York Times*, I had waited years for just such an opportunity as I was being handed. But instead of excitedly racing out into the street, I chose to stare out my window at the back of the Waldorf Astoria, and ponder the meaning of foreign service life. I especially wondered what exactly was going to be in it for me.

What do I do with my life now, I asked myself, now that I had given up (gladly, I had thought) my career as a television journalist? The alternatives, in those early days as an accompanying spouse, seemed limited to over-eating, crying, throwing things at the television set when news actors presented the news, and desperately feeling like my world had collapsed. I had forgotten altogether that my friends thought I was the luckiest woman alive.

'NOTHING TO DO' SYNDROME

Unknown to me at the time, since I was still a neophyte in my new role and lifestyle, I was falling victim to a fate which I would have shared with the colonial ladies of the British Raj. Not only did their experience give rise to their official designation (along with children) of the 'useless mouths' (I tried to use that on my passport application), but they also put a name to a condition thousands of traveling wives to follow would suffer from: 'nothing to do' syndrome.

You certainly don't have to travel to suffer from it. But in an international setting, where there may be hot and cold running servants attending to your basic needs, your husband and children are gone for the day, your house is decorated institutionally, and it's stifling hot or freezing cold outside your door, you may in fact sit down in a chair with a day stretching before you which has too many hours to fill.

Compounding matters further can be the early hour at which your foreign city awakens and begins its day. In many hot countries, life shuts down for rests or siestas after lunch and in temperate countries, winter afternoons are as black as night. Some days will feel endless and empty.

It's true that while you are settling in, there are countless numbers of errands to occupy many of those hours. And if you have moved to a Western country and are facing daily life without servants for the first time, you may feel like there will never be any personal free time again in this century. But when the last picture has been hung on the wall of your new home, the last piece of furniture purchased, the last drawer organized to perfection, the last child settled in school for the entire day or for just a few hours, or a routine finally established which frees you for at least a few hours a day, it is hard to avoid facing up to the next stage in your overseas adventure: Now what do I do with myself?

EVERYBODY ASKS THEMSELVES THIS QUESTION

First off, if you are pondering the 'now what' question, be aware that you are not alone. Some may wonder about it for a minute, others for the length of the entire posting, but most wives who move abroad with their husbands will at some point ask themselves what they should do next. All the pre-planning in the world, all the enthusiasm for the local culture and people, won't clear up the existential angst of the early days. Unlike the working half of the couple, the spouse's life is completely uncharted and open to suggestion. I'm not talking here about the responsibilities associated with children, because they don't change no matter where you live in the world. They go with any territory.

Rather, I'm referring to free time, the personal time to pursue whatever interests you, and only you. For some women, this could mean finding the nearest bridge game or golf course. For others, it could be volunteering at the local welfare home or cultural society. Still others will want to check out the local job market. Before you head off with your golf clubs or résumé, there will still likely be a moment when you draw a blank – call it a dead time zone, or whatever you prefer – where you may find yourself sitting in a chair, staring out a window and contemplating your new universe. You want to get moving on something new, but can't seem to find the mental energy.

Worse still, you may be immobilized by the cultural stereotypes which await you outside your door. A Hong Kong Chinese woman I know who moved to the United States, said she preferred to do nothing all day rather than face new people who reduced her to the cultural stereotype of a passive Chinese woman, content to be a mere toy for her Western husband. When this same woman moved to Taiwan, it bothered her even more to have people assume she married not for love, but for a U.S. passport.

If you feel like hiding out for the duration of your post, don't despair: you aren't the first woman to be immobilized by apathy or stereotyping.

Before you can get to the point where you can overcome your own inertia, be aware that there may be many contributing factors you haven't considered. Some of them are unique to overseas life – like finding good help to keep the dust from the Gobi desert off your furniture, or incompatible electric currents, or just plain exhaustion from the move itself.

If you ignore these factors, and are just too hard on yourself, you risk not only prolonging your lethargy, but giving yourself a massive dose of depression on top of it all. Before you can get on with your new life abroad, you may first have to recognize and deal with a few feelings which are downright impossible to avoid.

AGE AND STAGE OF BOREDOM

A lot of the structured activities in your overseas life will depend on the age and stage of your life. If you have young children with you, it can be easier to not only plug into the community faster (by virtue of necessity) but also find that the last thing you are suffering from is 'nothing to do' syndrome. For the young mother, there will likely be not enough hours in the day to do everything you want to do (like relax, put your feet up for five minutes, and remember you are actually living abroad).

In the beginning, feelings of intense boredom are more likely to overwhelm women without the responsibility of children. These spouses may find their husbands are out for long working days which stretch into evening entertainment, while she sits waiting at home, staring at a wall. Many places won't offer diversions like television, and houses may be so far apart that night driving is required. In such circumstances, it is critical to one's mental health to get focused on something which will keep the mind active. But first you'll have to get past a question swirling around in your brain...

...WHO AM I?

One of the biggest emotional headaches for spouses moving abroad, is the temporary loss of the critical qualities which a woman needs to keep her ego from collapsing in total despair – self-confidence, self-esteem and a sense of her own identity. In my experience, the first social invitation provides the litmus test for how those qualities are faring overseas. If you fail the test, you're in good company.

It doesn't matter if it's your first dinner party, cocktail party, or coffee morning, a good majority of women will decide at the last minute – that they don't want to go! I use an exclamation point only because it will match most women's emotional condition at the point of their decision. The reasons for the refusal will vary: nothing to wear, hair needs to be cut but a trustworthy hairdresser hasn't been found, a perm has gone awry in tropical heat, exhaustion and lack of energy, inability to reciprocate while still unsettled, or a face which is a mass of welts from allergic reactions to hotel soap. (I'm not making that one up. Honest.)

The list of excuses will go on and on but they will share a common theme. You feel rotten about yourself. You feel invisible and inferior. You hate yourself and nobody could possibly like you. You're not budging, ever, from your hotel room, apartment, or house.

If your husband is standing by watching your self-flagellation (I should ask my own husband to add a footnote here) he will either be shaking his head or trying not to laugh. But it isn't funny to you, especially if you can remember a time long ago when you were a confident person who felt good about herself. When we moved overseas our first time to Bangkok, it would be an understatement to say that my self-confidence was at an all-time low. I wanted to stand at parties and hand out my résumé as a way of showing people that I was certainly a more interesting person than I appeared to be – which was a sweating, self-conscious, newly-arrived wimpish looking character, clutching a sweaty purse, frozen three inches from the hors d'oeuvre table. Early after we arrived in Beijing (and I was supposedly getting good at moving around), I gave this post-arrival inferiority complex a name: 'speck syndrome'. Hi, I wanted to say and practically did, I'm nobody from nowhere: Ms. Speck of Dust.

It is the rare individual who can casually walk into a room to face strangers (even friendly ones) after just relocating her life thousands of miles. Absolutely nobody is that secure. It takes time to build up that security again.

When it dawns on you, however, that almost every woman who moves abroad must start from scratch and rebuild her shattered ego and actually manages to do so, your own self-confidence begins to return. You realize that like everyone else, you too will get past being the nervous newcomer. People will know who you are, remember meeting you or hearing about you from somebody else. Someone may actually remember that you have a skill of some sort and ask you to do something – bake a cake, give a course, perhaps a job offer. Events do eventually transpire to allow the return of your self-confidence.

In an overseas setting, though, you must make more of an effort. There is no built-in security blanket of friends or family, or even professional community like you may have had at home. You have to be more aggressive and open with people; ask questions, follow up with phone calls to arrange another meeting. Try thinking of your ego like the stock market – it hasn't crashed, but rather, it is going through adjustments, and will even out given the proper circumstances. Often, just one new friend with common interests, or an assignment of any kind, will set you on track again.

My Hong Kong Chinese friend, for instance, quickly realized that she would have to compromise a bit and attempt to be more outgoing than she would normally be at home. She also befriended a Filipino woman while living in Taiwan. Together they faced many of the same attitude problems and could empathize with each other. Your self-esteem will be challenged throughout your posting, just as it can be at home, but a foreign setting can inflame inferiority complexes, and it won't just be successful women in the host culture who throw your self-image into the gutter.

Often, other expatriate women, who exude confidence and ability, will get you down, especially when you are starting out in your new post and feeling unsure of yourself. You may meet some dynamo who has started her own export business of some rare local treasure, and you haven't even been able to find raisins anywhere. On my first posting, when I still believed I wanted to be a foreign correspondent (motherhood helped me abandon that fantasy), I met real live female foreign reporters one day and felt so inadequate telling them I was writing articles for airline magazines that I wanted to slide under the lunch table. Since I was extremely pregnant at the time, it was a physical impossibility, but I would gladly have disappeared by magic if I'd been capable.

Self-confidence and self-esteem do return overseas, but have to be nurtured slowly and deliberately. The first time you go out and do something by yourself, you gain both confidence in your abilities to function in a new city and a better feeling about yourself. The trick is to attempt something relatively easy, thereby guaranteeing success. I am not making this up: on our second posting, just the simple act of successfully purchasing a box of paper clips in a downtown Taipei stationery store boosted my morale enormously (to say nothing of my skills at charades). Take small steps at first.

It is also very difficult for even the most energetic of souls to project an identity separate from her husband's when you are settling into a posting. After all, his job is still the main event no matter how busy you get. He has all the instant status. Yours will come in time. So in the beginning, accept that you are Mrs. Banking Corporation, or Mrs. Second Secretary and be patient for the return of your own credibility as an individual. What's important is that *you* know who you are, not some stranger you may never see again in your life. I realize this is easier said than done but it's a terrific character building exercise to begin measuring your self-worth in your own eyes rather than in someone else's. Returning home with that ability under your belt, will also be a lot more useful than some trinket you'll have to dust every second day.

If you have kept your maiden name rather than take your husband's, now is not the time to change it. Keep your own name. Some women revert to married names overseas because they think it's simpler to explain who they are. The quickest way to lose your own identity is to give up the name you've been used to for the past number of decades. In many countries, it is the custom for women to keep their maiden names, so you wouldn't be that unusual. And sometimes, last names get lost in the shuffle anyway. For most of my first posting in Thailand, I was known as Mrs. Robin (or a close approximation) so switching to a married name would have served no purpose, except fuel my identity crisis.

One last comment about identities: print up name cards for yourself that don't mention your spouse. Not only are name cards a great way to get home in a taxi (if you have the card printed in the local language on one side) but they are also proof positive that you exist outside of your marriage – in print at least.

...SPEAKING OF YOUR MARRIAGE

The dynamics of your marriage may very well change when you move overseas, and you will find yourself simultaneously adapting to not only a new country but also to a new role as spouse which you didn't play at home. Not only will the host country view you in a completely different light from what you may be used to, but your spouse may also suddenly heap expectations upon you which were not part of your original nuptial agreement.

If you are the wife of a businessman or diplomat who is expected to host a lot of official entertainment, you may suddenly be playing chatelaine of a large household and staff, organizing cocktail receptions or sit-down dinner parties for twelve. If you are married to a foreign aid worker, you could be thrust into life in poverty-stricken villages in which your spouse expects you to organize a women's weaving cooperative. While some women find such opportunities challenging, not everyone is suited for them, and arguments over just what is expected of you as Mrs. Whatever Organization, could get heated.

Likewise, child-care responsibilities, which may have been egalitarian at home, may change when you move to a foreign country. The husband may be expected to 'officially' play golf on Saturday or Sunday mornings, leaving you to entertain the children for the day. Or in the presence of so many servants, the working partner may suddenly decide to take a powder since help is on the scene, despite your pleas that a maid is not a parent. Likewise, a husband used to servants back home may fail to notice that the wife he just transplanted into a servantless Western society is looking pretty weary from her new unasked-for role as household maid.

Further disagreements can break out if you decide to work and your new job interferes with your spouse's. After all, you may very well be reminded, you have not moved thousands of miles for *your* job and seething resentment will lie behind your smile (if you're capable of one) while you attempt to cancel your plans or rearrange your life to reach a so-called compromise definitely not in your favor. Or perhaps you haven't worked since the children were born, and suddenly your husband – thrust into a Western society which necessitates two incomes – is hinting none too subtly about you getting a part-time job.

Expectations of just what will be required of you overseas must be hammered out before you leave home, and then renegotiated regularly once you are living abroad. Keep the lines of communication open and honest. I told my diplomat husband that under no circumstances would I go to cocktail parties unless they were of particular interest to me. For one thing, they are fattening (especially when you glue yourself to the food table), and for another, I hate getting all dressed up for an occasion which lasts less than two hours at which nobody is likely to even ask me once what I do. So over the years, my husband and I have reached an agreement which satisfies my waistline and my ego. I rarely go to official functions.

If you plan to work, parameters must be set with your spouse and your employer to avoid disputes. You can't maintain any credibility if you take on the responsibilities of a job only to inform your employer that your spouse feels a dinner party has to take precedence over an assigned task. The credibility of working 'accompanying' spouses is already stretched in some foreign communities and you ruin it for serious professional women if you fly the coup to rush home to prepare hors d'oeuvre.

Like many other aspects of living abroad, extra effort must be put into marriage because there are tensions and circumstances which can be very different from home. The ladies of the British Raj, for instance, very often found themselves married to men who suddenly went from modest, humble fellows back home in England, to self-important, aggrandizing obnoxious chaps overseas (and that may have only been a man low on the Raj totem pole). Let's just say I've seen evidence that some things haven't changed much since colonial service. Be on the lookout for inflated egos so that compromises can be reached and everyone's feet can remain firmly planted on the ground.

DELICATE CONDITIONS AND HYPOCHONDRIA
World health conditions have improved, but it is still true that you could occasionally pick up some rare disease when you move abroad. More often, however, spouses fall victim to one known side effect of 'nothing to do' syndrome, one certainly well-documented by the ladies of the Raj. That is, the collapse of otherwise hearty women into delicate creatures.

Admittedly, women of the 19th century weren't expected to appear as sturdy as they actually were, but an account in an 1830 journal of one woman of the Raj's experience in India noted that "...most Englishwomen in India in the Early Raj days had entirely given up walking. They either rode on horseback or were carried about in palanquins."

Before you dismiss such laziness as a condition of the last century, consider there may be a 20th century replacement in many overseas posts: the driver. Having lived in busy, congested cities where complete anarchy reigns in traffic, and driving yourself around is admittedly suicidal, I still believe that driver lethargy is a condition which befalls many an accompanying spouse. What should be used as a convenience (for grocery shopping, picking up children from school, navigating difficult districts) can quickly become a replacement for using your own two legs to walk two feet to buy milk. A new city becomes familiar and more interesting from the ground level, so, even with a driver in your employ, walking should be considered occasionally to keep the body and mind not only healthier, but rooted in the real world as well.

Unnecessary medical appointments, while certainly providing something to do, can get tedious after a while, to say nothing of costly. Before you leave home, make sure you're healthy enough to live abroad and save yourself the trouble of moving if you're not. At the same time, don't be alarmed if you feel like you're falling apart in small ways when you are first settling in. It's natural to react in non-life threatening ways to new food, a new lifestyle, and new smells. You're not going crazy. Your body will even itself out after a while and let you function again as a normal human being.

CULTURE AFTERSHOCKS

Many of those small non-debilitating illnesses may also be a result of the second stage of culture shock mentioned in chapter three. Once you get past the honeymoon phase (where you think everything is marvelous about your new environment), your mood may come tumbling down into complete hostility towards all that surrounds you. When you are in such a frame of mind, it is not surprising that your body may react in subtle, and not-so-subtle ways.

Fears of your new environment, which may not have been that strong upon arrival, may grow when you realize that you are in fact staying and not returning home. Traffic, dirty streets, or anything which may have seemed quaint at the beginning, suddenly becomes impossible to bear a minute longer, or frightens you from stepping out into the street. It becomes a case less of having nothing to do, and more of being afraid to do anything at all. Many of these fears are also symptoms of culture shock and will disappear after a while like every other phase of your move abroad.

SO WHAT DO I DO?

It's hard to get someone else motivated, but I can offer some of the strategies I've used on myself which work – sometimes.

☞ Make Yourself at Home

When it finally sinks into your mind that wherever you are, it is to stay for a while, you can do yourself a big favor and start feeling like you are at home, and not in some transitory place. There's no greater impediment to getting on with things than feeling like you'll only be somewhere for a short time, so why bother getting started. So get used to your new digs as quickly as possible. Tell yourself that you are finished puttering around with decorations and essential errands. When you feel that something is unfinished, it gets in the way of moving onto the next project. So go ahead, pick up your purse and go out the door. Join the local library; volunteer at the welfare home; take up that sewing course; register for the aerobics class; go for that facial; *get on* with your new life.

☞Homesickness can be Counter-Productive

Sure, it would be nice to be home for a variety of reasons, but you aren't there and the sooner you stop acting like Dorothy in the *Wizard of Oz* (there's no place like home) the better off you will feel. As a Canadian who lives in the countryside, my heart aches in September when I know the leaves are changing back home while I stare at trees with leaves which never seem to drop, never mind change their color. I try to let the longing wash over me like a nice dream, and then wake up and get on with my life at hand. I don't always succeed, but as I tell my young daughter, even mommies aren't perfect. At least I try. You should too.

☞Set Priorities on Your Time

When you have difficulties getting started with your new routine, it can often be due to an overwhelming sense of time commitments to spouse, children, volunteer organizations, and then finally, yourself. In some foreign settings, time becomes fractured due to schedules compounded by the level of difficulty in navigating the city. On our second posting in Taiwan, for instance, traffic made a trip into the downtown area from the expatriate district at least a three-hour affair (and that gave you about twenty minutes for whatever you were trying to do). Because my children were young and I was on duty every few hours for a pickup or delivery, I rarely saw the inner city.

If this kind of set-up happens to you, one positive step to get over feeling distracted by a fractured time frame, is to sit down and figure out how much time you want – or need – to give to all the activities critical in your life. Don't be dismayed if you find personal time only limited to twenty or thirty-minute stretches. It is amazing what one can do despite time constraints.

☛Get Your Mind off Yourself

Stop worrying about things you can't change. In this instance, I don't just mean your new environment. I mean your body, your unruly hair, or your personality. Focus outward and look around you rather than getting self-absorbed, which I know is extraordinarily easy to do when you're feeling sorry for yourself. If you want to change something, think about going after that which you can change, like your skills, or your knowledge about your host culture.

TWO ROADS DIVERGED

It is my opinion that when you move abroad, you are presented with two fundamental choices. You can choose to be either a cool spectator or an active participant in your new culture.

The latter option doesn't necessarily have to mean studying hundreds of hours to become fluent in a foreign tongue, or going native completely. It could just mean not sitting on the sidelines (or in a rented apartment) and wasting a golden opportunity which you will most certainly later regret.

Not everyone will start a lucrative business, or begin a new career when they live overseas. But most people do have the capability of walking out their door and opening their eyes to soak in the colors, rhythms, customs, even just the street life of a foreign city.

If you think there is nothing to do, think again.

Chapter Five

CAREERS CAN TRAVEL TOO
Success Depends on Your State of Mind

**"I can sympathize with some of these wives,"
I said. "They get married right out of
college, the husband gets an overseas post
and everything's fine – the woman becomes a
hostess. Then she sees that what she's really
doing is boosting her husband in his job.
What's in it for her?"**

—from the story 'The Dependent Wife'
The Consul's File, by Paul Theroux

My friends may not believe this, but in recent years I have
calmed down considerably when contemplating the notion of
working abroad. No longer does my pulse quicken, my
patience fly out the window, and my general self-esteem
plummet when I consider that great philosophical query
known to most traveling wives, most especially professional
foreign service spouses: What the $%&*()(*&^ am I going to
do over there and can I make any money from it?

This is not to say that I have abandoned altogether my
ornery harangues of officials of any stripe who could possibly
employ wives overseas, or lobby for more moral support from
my own government's foreign outposts. I can still work up a
good sweat and go into my strident spouse routine on cue.
But somewhere along the line – I'd hate to think age and
motherhood may actually have had something to do with it –
I've gradually changed the way I view what I previously had
perceived as the rewards of a structured working life. In other
words, I've done some serious rethinking about what a 'career'
should really mean in the context of a mobile life.

WHAT EXACTLY IS A CAREER?

How you define the word 'career' in your own mind can make or break you. If you believe the word 'career' should include such notions as moving up a corporate ladder, pay raises, promotions, or even mentors, stop right there. As a traveling wife, the popular interpretation of the word 'career' is just out of sync with your life on the move. The structure necessary to promote those concepts just won't be there. There are no ladders, except those you climb to board an airplane in some foreign airfield. Your professional life is quite unique.

Consider instead a more appropriate definition of the word 'career', one which actually comes out of a dictionary to prove I'm not making this up to make you feel better. I found one such definition for the word 'career' to mean 'a path through life'.

When applied to women – traveling or not – this definition makes infinitely more sense. For on a path, there are no corporate checkpoints; no great rush. You can amble along, let people pass you by if they're in a hurry, or just stroll off the main path to see what lies down another winding trail. You can stop along a path; it may change in scenery and terrain, but no matter where you are in the world, it's still *your* path and not somebody else's. You are your own judge – there are no lifestyle writers hiding in the bushes waiting to jump out and chronicle your experiences for the women's pages. You alone gauge the distance you want to go.

WHAT IS A MOBILE CAREER?

Well, it's your own path. One which you can jump onto anywhere in the world and feel at home. You set your own pace, and most important of all, you use all the talents which make you unique. When you see the path as one for an entire life – not merely a short stop until the next promotion – you aren't limiting yourself to one vocation. Everything you do becomes part of your career: from raising children, to foreign travel, to working at a variety of jobs.

Instead of presuming that moving abroad means you are giving up the skills you trained for, recognize that on a life-long career path you will not only pick up new skills, but also discover ones you never suspected you had. In a mobile career, different skills become useful at different times. Your options are limitless, not limited.

Working outside of a structure gives you more flexibility. You can accommodate distractions peculiar to overseas life – home leave, exotic holidays, visitors from home. The only obstacles to a successful mobile career in these newly defined terms, are inapplicable expectations.

ADJUSTING YOUR CAREER EXPECTATIONS AND VALUES

Ask yourself what constitutes a successful career. Is it money? Prestige? High profile? Once again, in a traveling life, those values simply may not apply so why bother torturing yourself trying to achieve the impossible?

Materialistic measuring sticks, like money, are often so inappropriate on a foreign posting – especially if you are posted to a Third World country where you will likely begin to view materialism in a new light. I don't advocate working for nothing. I believe that if you are a professional, you should be paid – something. But if a job appeals to you, don't turn it down because the pay isn't what you expected it to be. Try to determine new ways of measuring and evaluating success which are appropriate to your traveling life, and also to the stage and experience you have reached in living overseas.

On the first time out, you may need to find out what you are capable of doing. Your experience may be limited, so you may not be able to accomplish all that you want to do. On our first time abroad, I simply wasn't ready for my fantasy of foreign reporting. I was not only a neophyte in Asia, incapable of differentiating the warring factions in nearby Cambodia, I was also at the age when the idea of childbearing was most appealing.

Timing can be critical but this is often a lesson you learn the hard way. It would have been unrealistic for me to expect to run out and try to join *Time Magazine* when I lived in Bangkok but that's practically what I did, not only during our first year overseas, but in my seventh month of pregnancy. I had panicked over my professional life and upon hearing that *Time* might have needed a new stringer to work with the Bangkok-based correspondent, I foolishly made an appointment to meet him.

After walking over to the correspondent's home, and miscalculating the distance, I stood before him, my résumé and clippings limp in my hand from the humidity, watching his face evaluate and try to understand why the sweating bloated blob of a woman standing before him could conceivably want freelance work at such an advanced state of pregnancy. He obviously hadn't met many compulsive traveling female careerists.

If he had, he might have done a story about them. Still, I will always give the man credit for some compassion because he started telling me about the birth of his own Bangkok baby instead of completely humiliating me on the spot. And needless to say, he told me to come back after I'd had the baby and we would talk more comfortably then. I never set eyes on him again.

My advice? Go ahead and act like a possessed person about your career anyway. Try everything. Be rejected. Be disappointed. It truly does build character and helps you out in the long run. This advice is not intended to sound patronizing – because it's obviously coming from a formerly possessed person – but sometimes it doesn't hurt to get some things out of your system.

When I returned home from my 'interview' with *Time* I went to bed and wouldn't come out for two days. In the end, though, I was able to laugh at myself about it, and to use the experience to remind myself that sometimes, it pays to wait.

HOW DO I SPELL SUCCESS? NOT M*O*N*E*Y

Here's an exercise I devised for myself to help me develop a healthier (and happier) professional perspective on moving abroad.

When we were posted back to Canada after three years in Bangkok, I abandoned mainstream journalism for the most part, and switched over to selling my various communications skills. This meant I could work for a variety of people as either a scriptwriter or speechwriter; slide show producer or propaganda writer; communications strategist or any other lofty title I decided to assign myself.

Was I successful? That depends entirely on what I consider to be 'success'. In some of my work, notably my winning lucrative consultant's contracts from the Canadian government, I'll confess that money made me feel quite successful. But more important to me was achieving a working life which combined the flexibility of working from home and having children.

Upon hearing that we would be moving once again to the Far East for several years – and once again forcing me to not only start the process of building new contacts but also lose a substantial income – I admit I momentarily slipped into that horrible state of Total Despair which many women are familiar with.

The time for personal re-evaluation and reassessment of the meaning of 'success' vis-à-vis happiness abroad had clearly arrived.

In my view, the primary lesson I needed to learn to keep my sanity was how to teach myself to get away from viewing success in my crass, materialistic Western way: money. So I put this question to myself: Why will a major cut in pay actually be an advantage to me both personally and professionally? To my own surprise, I came up with several positive and satisfying answers by listing previously unarticulated, non-materialistic bonuses to life abroad.

I may take a pay cut, I told myself, but in return I will gain the following benefits:

1. Adventure, travel, exotica;
2. The opportunity to be creative (to write something other than government bafflegab);
3. An escape route from government bureaucracy and petty officials;
4. Enormous amounts of quality family time;
5. Cultural exposure and lessons of tolerance (which would also be terrific for my children);
6. Experience which may not translate into a job right away but will come in handy at a later date.

ASK YOURSELF WHY YOU WANT TO WORK OVERSEAS

Aside from money which we'd all love to make, it's important to truly understand your motives for wanting to seek work abroad. They will ultimately affect the decisions you make about the kind of work to pursue or accept.

If it is still money that you are after, you can forget about making it overseas unless you are a teacher and secure a position with the international schools (locally-engaged teachers aren't as highly paid as those hired from the home countries and then assigned abroad). Full-time positions with embassies other than your own are also not to be counted on. Jobs which do become open to expatriate wives usually pay a minimum wage. Determined to continue a career pattern started back home? Your choices of work overseas will be limited by local labor laws and to your particular field and that narrowly defined focus could limit your prospects for finding a job. However, it is not impossible especially if your expertise is relatively unique. An environmental expert I met in Beijing, who after months of what seemed like futile searching, finally connected with the right people and ended up with more work than she could possibly handle. But in the meantime, it may not hurt to seek out new dictionary definitions for the word 'compromise' and try to apply it to your life. You may have to adapt your focus to fit into a limited market. Business ventures, such as import/export, often pay off as well, but they do require meticulous market research and a sound financial support system.

If you set your goal at intellectual stimulation to keep from going crazy (I tend to choose this one overseas) your chances of success are considerably greater. Why? You broaden your options and chances of success. So many projects overseas can be stimulating by virtue of their novelty. It may only take one small, part-time project to succeed if intellectual excitement is your goal. It isn't measured by a pay-cheque; it can be obtained by meeting people or by reading material; it can be self-initiated; and very often can be done from home with a limited number of childcare arrangements if your children are still young. It also provides an answer to that dreaded of all questions occasionally asked of a spouse: "Are you working at something?"

I GAVE UP MY CAREER!

Probably the worst philosophical – and emotional – land mine a woman can face on a posting is the feeling that she has not only given up her career to be with her husband, but she has also given up the status and recognition which went with her profession. Before you can get onto the job of finding a job, you must first grapple with this identity crisis which many women before you have had to come to terms with. This is an issue which goes beyond the idea of making money, for often money is not enough. Respect. We all want it and often it takes a job to feel like we're getting enough of it.

There is no sure-fire advice I can offer a woman in the throes of this issue. Like flying long distance or unpacking endless boxes of kitchen gadgets, this is simply one that has to be endured. Finding a job or any situation which makes you feel happy and normal again, will naturally help your ego return to liveable standards, but until that day, it will be a hard task for many women to keep their emotions from jumping all over the place and for some, hitting rock bottom. In this instance, it helps to talk to as many women as possible, if only to reassure yourself that you aren't the first to go through it all. We all do. It is a facet of moving abroad which will never go away easily so just let it run its course.

MOTIVATION: DON'T LEAVE HOME WITHOUT IT

It's important that we all have our dreams of working. But remember that nothing, absolutely nothing, will happen to you overseas unless you make it happen. You must be willing to be a little bit afraid. There are going to be risks to working in a foreign environment, not the least of which will be a morbid fear of getting lost on the way to your interview.

I know that not everyone has the same level of adrenalin or chutzpa (or sheer foolhardiness) but everyone has a little. You've agreed to move overseas, haven't you? Some of your friends back home are likely telling you already they are in awe of your nerve.

Sitting in your new overseas home will not get you a job unless you are actively using the phone to find one. Eventually, you will have to go outside your door to look for work because nobody is going to hand you some nicely organized, structured 9–5 job. In foreign communities where such aberrations do exist, you will find yourself competing with hundreds of other spouses for the privilege of holding such a job.

All the skills in the world are useless to you unless you are motivated enough to pick up the phone, or write that letter, or seek out that individual whose name you were given by someone you don't know but whose son plays with your daughter and so on. If you think anyone is going to hand you something, especially your husband's employer, you'll be sorely disappointed.

The pressure to succeed and the feeling that finding a job is the only way to make your new life bearable, has a tremendous effect on your level of motivation. It will spur you into action. If aggressive behavior is frowned upon back in your own culture, you will surprise yourself on how quickly you will adapt to the ways of your host culture. When you truly want to find work, your adrenalin will start pumping. I've seen it over and over again from women from all sorts of different cultures.

NEVER AGREE TO ANYTHING BEFORE YOU GET THERE

Never, ever, agree to any job until you see your new home, city, country, environment, lay of the land. I've seen women run around half-possessed, lining up work for their posting from home with companies, governments, schools and other likely employers. They sign on the dotted line before they have any idea what their schedules will be like over there, nor do they know if they'll have transportation, how bad traffic is, what wages might be and so on. You can guess what I'm getting at here.

It may make great war stories to hear some wife tell you about how she started work the instant she arrived at post, but read between the lines – the stress lines all over her face.

I speak once again from experience. When we moved to Bangkok, the thought of being idle for even one minute depressed me so I instantly ran out and lined up a job doing what most expatriate wives desperate for work end up doing – teaching English. That's fine for someone with ESL training, or teaching experience. But for a journalist like myself, it was horrible. I hated it immediately and had to plot for four months afterwards how to get out of my commitment.

Yes, it would be nice to know in advance what you may do *over there* but give yourself time to unpack your boxes and figure out which end is up before plunging into work. Certainly explore possibilities with potential employers, but wait until the culture shock fog lifts from your head before racing across town in traffic to a job you're not sure you even want.

You may also need the time to set up childcare arrangements which satisfy everyone concerned. When your children are in school all day, it becomes a little easier to arrange time to work. If they are pre-schoolers, it could take a few months to sort out child care, activities and other related duties. I have worked from home since marrying into the foreign service and firmly believe it is one of the best options when your children are still young (or you are still producing them). When I lived in Canada between postings, I would drop my children off at a home day care when I needed to be away from home to attend a meeting.

Living in Beijing, or any other Third World country where servants are an affordable option, you can combine motherhood and work by assigning yourself a work area and teaching your children early on to respect your space. Of course it takes a bit of discipline to work from home, but consider the fringe benefits: you can still be there when they come home from school or wake up from their nap. And you aren't stuck in an office all day worrying how you will get the laundry or grocery shopping done. It can all be squeezed in with a little time management. And a supportive husband.

KNOW WHAT YOUR SKILLS ARE

It also doesn't hurt to have an inventory of your own skills. This is definitely something you can do before leaving home and finish off in the early days after your arrival overseas. Résumés, while useful, are never enough because they often don't reveal the full extent of your skills. They are also often more useful only after you've secured a job.

A good reference book to help you sort out the kinds of skills you may have is *What Color Is Your Parachute* by Richard Nelson Bolles. It offers practical advice, as does his abridged version, *The New Quick Job-Hunting Map*. Another good source of information on skills and job hunting is a magazine called *Working Woman*. It doesn't normally include features on working overseas, but it does offer sensible how-to advice on writing business letters and résumés.

Bolles divides skills into three main areas: skills with people (including animals), with information (sometimes called data), or skills with things. Skills which involve people and information are particularly useful for people on the move.

Some of the skills involving people, according to Bolles, include: working with animals, training, counseling, advising and consulting, treating, founding and leading, negotiating and deciding, managing and supervising, performing and amusing, persuading, communicating, sensing, feeling, serving and finally, taking instructions.

Skills with information and data include: achieving, expediting, planning and developing, designing, creating, synthesizing, improving, adapting, visualizing, evaluating, organizing, analyzing, researching, computing, copying, storing, retrieving, comparing, and observing. Using those suggestions, try making a list of your own skills.

IT TAKES MORE THAN SKILLS: BE CREATIVE

I've already mentioned that motivation is essential to a satisfying professional life overseas. Now add to that a large dose of creativity. In most cases abroad, you must create your own opportunities and market your own skills. You must dream up creative ways of selling yourself. Admittedly, it often takes an outsider to see the creative possibilities for someone else.

I was having lunch one day in Taipei with a newly arrived nurse who told me she was especially interested in herbal, holistic medicine. We chatted a bit about Chinese natural medicines, when she told me she had met a Chinese doctor who had actually expressed an interest in her working for him, in his pharmacy no less, on a part-time basis. She couldn't quite decide what to do. So I offered the suggestion that she negotiate something part-time in order to learn from this doctor about Chinese medicines, which in my view, when compiled, would make a great handbook for the foreigners of Taipei. I know she went out to see the doctor the next day, and while some perfect scenario may not have come of it right away, she was beginning to see that there were possibilities with a little bit of creativity.

In Beijing, I met each week with three other women with whom I had formed an ad hoc support group. We sat around drinking too many cups of coffee, listening and evaluating each other's ideas for working. There doesn't have to be a common theme to your work fantasies either: my support group consisted of one former Taiwanese journalist, one Harvard-educated environmental lawyer (my friend, the environmental expert), one budding published self-help book writer (guess who) and one entrepreneurial free spirit who beat all of us to the marketplace with Chinese peasant painting T-shirts which sold like hot cakes by her first Christmas in Beijing.

Here are a few ideas to get you started:

☛Work the Internet

Not only has the Internet allowed expats to stay in touch with one another, it has been a boon for spouses wishing to pursue careers overseas or stay in touch or up to date with the one they left behind.

Telecommuting, the idea that you can work entirely over the Internet from anywhere in the world, is a new work reality and one which expat spouses might want to consider. Check out http://www.escapeartist.com, a huge expat site that has links to many telecommuting job sites. Likewise, there are now giant career boards placed on the Internet, which can give you ideas and leads. Freelance writing, an area I pursued all over the place, is now much easier to get into, thanks to e-mail and the Internet's on-line 'zines. Check out travel sites to see what information or articles you may be able to contribute from your posting.

☛If you like to shop

My father came to visit us when we lived in Bangkok and offered this suggestion to me after he watched me buzz around the city on my millionth shopping tour with the visiting friend of a friend of a friend who was given our Bangkok phone number. "You should be a personal shopping guide for tourists," he suggested. "But I don't know the language very well," I responded. "Hasn't stopped you from shopping and helping so many others buy their way across Bangkok has it?" He was right. I didn't have the time myself for this enterprise (although I did write an article for Thai International which put my own tour into print so others could follow it) but I think the idea is a good one. Once again, business cards should be printed and foreign hotels approached. Often, visiting women would prefer the company of a fellow countrywoman to show her where the good buys are, or a good hairdresser, lunch spot, etc. Women who know the city well – and where to shop – could become these freelance shopping guides.

☛If you like to travel

It takes a lot of experience and certain skills to be a good travel agent, but if you end up doing a lot of traveling around your region, you may be in a position to freelance your travel advice to established agencies.

Most agents go out on familiarization trips which can't possibly include everything, and you may be able to offer reports on alternative accommodation, restaurants, tours, activities for children etc, which those agents weren't able to see in a short trip. Try local agents first, then suggest your availability to agencies in your home town.

FOCUS, FOCUS, FOCUS

Let me share a lesson I learned as a freelance journalist. When I would approach a publication I was anxious to write for, I learned very quickly that it wasn't enough for me to simply inform an editor that I would like to write for his magazine. Write what? the editor would wonder, before filing my letter in the nearest wastebasket. Instead, I learned to write 'query' letters which made specific story suggestions, and usually not just one but several.

In other words, after reading a magazine I wanted to write for (another lesson, know your market or organization you are approaching) I would suggest an article idea which I knew he could likely use. My very first published article in the Far East was the shopping tour I mentioned earlier. I had written in my query letter that since Bangkok was known as a man's haven, why not publish a piece about the ways in which a woman could indulge herself with manicures and fine silk outfits. That focused idea became 'A Woman In Bangkok' – a shopping and eating guide to Bangkok.

Naturally, we all don't know exactly what we want to do, but having some ideas worked out (a simple, "I'd like to work with children" may yield leads) will prove invaluable to you when you meet someone and investigate the possibilities of plugging into a project. The key to someone hiring you is by making sure (a) someone decides that they need a certain kind of service for their business or organization; and (b) you, and nobody else, are the person to provide that service.

PREPARE YOUR OWN PERSONAL MARKETING STRATEGY

Imagine this. A former top management consultant, executive, or just intelligent woman, is going overseas for the first time with her husband. At home, that individual worked for years managing several employees, overseeing expensive administrative budgets, or designing and implementing complicated projects of any description. The individual was known to be cool under pressure, strong in her judgement skills, and confident of her own abilities.

Someone asks her what she will do overseas, and despair, confusion or a combination of both cross her face. She's at a temporary loss. So the individual is asked: why not apply all those management skills to yourself? Instead of planning a mega-project, plan your own employment future using the same variables. Context, goals, roles of various players, time constraints, budget considerations, deadlines, target audience, marketing potential....An idea is born.

YOUR HUSBAND'S ORGANIZATION: STAY CLEAR

How can I put this nicely? I can't, so let me use a comparison. My advice on traveling on airplanes with small children always points out that some stewardesses tend to treat you as something akin to a leper. Sure, they are supposed to offer assistance, hand out toys, guarantee certain seating, etc., but I advise people never to count on anything. If a stewardess is nice, think of it as a bonus.

The same principle applies to your husband's organization, whether it be a bank, a government, or small business venture. If there are individuals ready to hire spouses – ready to think of a spouse in terms of her professional skills rather than merely the expensive luggage accompanying the employee – consider yourself lucky.

It's usually against a company's policy to hire a spouse overseas for all sorts of trumped up reasons: conflict of interest, husband and wife teams won't work – you get the picture. In some cases, it's the top ranking official's wife who doesn't want to see another wife in the office fulltime. I'm not being bitchy, either. I've seen a lot of that.

If you feel like trying your luck, though, here's a piece of advice. When you switch hats from accompanying spouse to professional, be professional. Arrange meetings during office hours, with résumés and proposals. State your objectives and pay expectations or working hours clearly. Don't drop in the office with a child in tow to chat about business or hit someone up at a party. If you want to be treated like a professional, act like one.

But make sure you have enough anti-high blood pressure medication, because take it from someone who knows. It's a sucker's game.

STICK TO OUTSIDE TARGETS

Universities, institutions, non-governmental organizations are often good hiring grounds in Third World countries. Likewise, multilateral organizations such as the United Nations and World Bank often hire locally. International offices of companies from back home, such as trade offices or chambers of commerce are also worth a gambit.

Never pass by a bulletin board anywhere without stopping. The yellow pages of a telephone book are a good spot to find counterpart companies: if you've been a management consultant or copywriter, see what's listed locally and make a few cold calls. Start with what you know best. That is, a health care worker should approach hospitals; musicians approach music schools and so on. Instead of just trying to answer newspaper employment advertisements, try placing one about yourself in the local English newspaper or city magazine.

THE HASSLE FACTOR

After a few personal work experiences which left me wrung out emotionally, I developed a litmus test to assess what I call the hassle factor of any potential job, and not just overseas. First things first: no matter how straightforward a project may sound, absolutely nothing is easy in a country which is foreign to you. People never do business the same way you do back home, so always be prepared to learn a few lessons along the way.

You may accept a job or contract, and only discover later that it can be a complicated process in order to get to the people you need to see, interview, or meet. They may have no phone, or their office is two buses and three rickshaw rides away. If you're a Westerner, they'll assume you have a driver.

Or how about this: you are hired to do one job only to find out that in actual fact, they would like you to do ten others, and will call you at all hours with more requests or want up-to-the-minute progress reports.

Language is another hassle factor, as very often the English spoken in the host country doesn't sound like the English we know. Like the time I got a call one day out of the blue from an editor associated with the American Medical Association. Would I be interested in attending a medical convention being held in Bangkok? All I would have to do, it was explained to me, was take notes of the proceedings. Easy enough, I thought, without thinking it through. I can even use my tape recorder.

The esteemed doctors had gathered in a local five-star hotel. Although I didn't recognize any names, it sure looked impressive to me. And then the first speaker addressed the gathering.

I leaned forward to hear better because it sounded like a foreign language. No. It was English. Except English was so obviously not this particular doctor's mother tongue, nor was it the first language of the second, third and fourth speakers down the line. They were making valiant efforts and so was I until I was as white as the paper on my lap. There was no way I could understand a single word, never mind the complicated medical jargon they were using. I had to abandon ship.

Consider every potential assignment very carefully. Ask yourself a few questions: Where will you be working? Will you be paid in this century? Will you have to bargain for your fee? (I had to once, unexpectedly, with a Thai cabinet minister I was writing English speeches for. Not the job, incidentally, I had been hired to do.)

THE IMPORTANCE OF NETWORKING

In the overseas context, networking is not just connecting for yourself. It's helping others connect, too, because at this particular juncture in your working life, cutthroat competition, back-stabbing, and office politics are themes which are not only inappropriate, they are counterproductive as well. Overseas, you have to be a lot nicer.

Sound crazy? Not when you consider how important support groups become when you move abroad. From mothers' organizations, to addiction groups, to just plain women who like to sew but can't find the right materials organizations, women find they need each other a lot more than they might at home. It's true we all know a few women we'd like to throw out a window, but when you stop and give every woman the benefit of the doubt, you will find it takes you a lot further in your relationships overseas.

When you live far away from home, and need to make friends and connections, you won't get very far by being a pill. You need to rediscover your basic nicer self in the absence of that hype and competition back home which may have thrown you off balance too much of the time, making you act too often in your own – and only your own – interest.

That kind of strategy just won't work overseas because it's difficult to operate in a vacuum. So, when listening around or asking about different jobs, think about whether you know someone else who may fit the bill if it's not for you. What goes around comes around, or so the saying goes. You can help yourself by helping others in the work game, and discover a few joys of friendship in the bargain. The women in the support group I was part of in Beijing, not surprisingly, became my best friends.

YOU WILL COME HOME AGAIN

Allow me to return again to my metaphor for 'career' as a path through life. That path, despite all its detours, may eventually take you home again so it's wise to plan ahead for what may lie down the road. This can be accomplished by asking yourself a few basic questions: Can I do this back home? When at home, ask it in reverse: Can I do this while I'm away?

I was lucky to have writing skills which transfer easily, but mine aren't the only ones which can be mobile. In particular, here are a few other portable ideas: anything which can be done from home on a self-employment basis such as computer skills, word processing, accounting, writing, editing, creative pursuits, public relations, photography, small business ventures, catering, management consulting, briefing other expatriates about adaptation, or being the 'point' person for visiting delegations of anything.

Outside the home, consider the health care industry, teaching, social services like counseling, office management, international development, English as a Second Language, private tutoring, fund-raising, museum and art gallery functions, and the hotel and travel industries.

BE TRUE TO YOURSELF

Above all else, don't change professions to keep up with your husband. When my husband went into foreign service, some friends asked me if I would too. Are you kidding? Me a diplomat? Never mind that I would have been laughed out of the examination room (I once wrote law boards and thought my results would tell me I have the intelligence of a fly). I reminded my friends that I was a journalist and a writer. If my husband wanted to learn to speak Chinese, that was his business. I'd stick to just eating Chinese food.

So my final word on this subject is this: try to go after something professional which offers mobility, but in all cases be true to your own talents and your own dreams. I'm convinced that if you are happy doing your own thing, following your own unique path in life wherever it may take you, you can be happy wherever you are in the world.

Chapter Six

MAIDS AND MADAMES
The Mixed Blessing of Servants

The mixed blessing of servants is simple: they are there when you want them, but also when you *don't* want them.

How could I possibly not want them? I wondered when briefed about servants before going on our first assignment. How could I not want someone around who was prepared to wash my clothes every day? Iron my husband's shirts? Change dirty diapers on my future babies? Cook for me every night? I knew it sounded too good to be true, but could the down side of such full-time assistance with my life really be that terrible? The person briefing me, a professional traveling wife of many years' experience, just smiled and said, "Wait. You'll see it's not all a bed of roses."

It took me less than two days to discover the thorn. The first day was terrific. We had just arrived at our Bangkok apartment when a Thai maid took the groceries from my hand, disappeared into the kitchen and shortly after placed a delicious platter of Thai rice before us for lunch.

Our shipment hadn't even arrived yet with our dishes and pots and pans, but 'madame' as I was to be known during my stay in Thailand, didn't have to concern herself anymore with such trivial matters. I was just to sit back and enjoy.

The next morning at dawn, when 'master' went off to report to the embassy (which opened at 7 a.m.) and 'madame' was depressed out of her mind because a long day of nothing lay ahead, I discovered my Thai maid had made my bed before I could crawl back into it. Then, while I sat staring into space on the living room couch, she was staring blankly at me while she vacuumed around my feet before setting off to the market to buy my food. I was becoming more suicidal by the second at the thought of a full-time audience for my mood swings, to say nothing of the guilt I felt from watching her do everything I hated to do myself, in return for a slave wage scale. The scene pushed my guilt barometer over the edge. Servants weren't just a mixed blessing, I cried to myself. They were going to be a curse.

SERVANT CULTURE SHOCK

I had read enough trashy novels with a Far East setting to recognize what was happening to me, but I had been temporarily distracted by the exhaustion of jet lag. Like other newcomers to the Third World, I was suffering from the shock of moving to a culture where life was cheap, the labor supply abundant, and anybody – certainly not just the privileged – could have a houseful of servants for a relatively low price. Even some servants in Thailand had servants.

If you've never allowed anyone other than a cleaning lady or your mother to see your messy closet, you may be in for a shock the first time you return home and find a maid, amah, aya, ayi, house-boy, nanny, helper, whoever ironing your husband's underwear. After the blush dies down on your face (especially if it's not even your maid doing the ironing, but a visiting friend of hers, which was the case for me) you'll begin to feel guilty for making her do all the dirty work you don't want to do. Such as ironing, cleaning vegetables, or straightening up your children's toys. You'll wonder how she can stay so good-natured considering what you're paying her.

All of these doubts come with servant culture shock. It's a condition only expatriates, especially those from developed countries who move to Third World countries can understand. Back home you may have had help, but you paid through the nose for it, and your helper was certainly not referred to as a servant. In some overseas settings, people come and go in your house or apartment and are clearly in charge of areas of responsibility you once called your own: your children, cupboards and pantry. Suddenly, you feel like your status has been elevated as high as a character in Masterpiece Theater, except this is not some nineteenth century drama.

On the other hand, expatriates from some Third World countries who are used to having household help suddenly find they have to do everything for themselves when they move to a Western country and that can be equally disconcerting. Or a woman used to treating her servants like members of the family may find herself in a country like China where helpers are assigned by the government and require an entirely different method of handling. Far from letting a servant go off and do their chores, a woman may discover that instructions must be given explicitly on a daily basis.

One way a woman can guage if she is reacting to the idea of having servants for the first time in her life (and mothers don't count) is the sudden onslaught of a mixture of good and evil thoughts running frantically through her mind. That is, at the same time that she's guilt-ridden, she is also secretly thrilled every time the maid calls her 'madame,' 'memsahib,' or, my favorite title while living in Taipei: 'missy.' The guilt phase quickly passes and before you know it, you're being waited on like everyone else. Worse still, you're likely bitching to your friends, the other madames, that your maid shows no initiative, needs to be shown how to do things, or her culinary skills (despite being a whiz at the local food) are just not up to scratch. You get used to having a maid, provided you've found a good one.

HIRING A SERVANT

I've been thrown into several different situations – the situation I described in Bangkok where my maid apparently came with the apartment; the kind where you need to find help yourself; and the worst situation of all, where servants are assigned to you with little or no choice on your part. That last option, which naturally occurred in the People's Republic of China, is the worst of all worlds but can still have a happy ending, if you're lucky.

In most Third World countries you plug into what I call the 'servant network.' You usually find that most amahs or maids in any given city have a network of friends whose names they are ready to provide on request. When you need to hire someone, you simply ask your friend's maid if they have a friend in need of a job. If that comes up dry, women's clubs or social organizations usually have bulletin boards with leads, especially as the time you arrive is normally a turnover period of personnel. Someone is bound to be advertising the fact that their help (wonderful with children) is now available.

Often, an embassy or company has a roster of servants who have been employed by staff over the years and are used to certain expatriate ways of living. It's not unusual for staff to be handed down for ten years or more to rotational staff. These are always the best kind of helpers, for not only will they be loyal and sensitive to your particular ethnic quirks, but they will also likely be able to tell you about all the people who have served in your company or embassy for the past decade. Remember every time your maid tells a story about a previous employer, that you'll be the next topic of conversation when you leave.

WHO TO HIRE

When we arrived in Taipei on our second posting, with a two-year-old in tow, I hired our amah even before we had left the hotel for our permanent quarters. We had plugged into the amah network early, and were fortunate to have a gem of a woman sent over immediately to meet us. Of course, I didn't know that she was a gem at the time, but it helped when she pulled out of her purse a photo album showing pictures of herself and the children she had looked after for the past thirty years. I knew I was meeting a pro.

I was so anxious to get out for a few hours – alone with my husband – that I decided that unless I took an instant dislike to the woman, I would bolt the minute my kids seemed comfortable. Luckily for us, I liked her immediately and my first impressions turned out to be correct. We went out for a short two-hour supper at a nearby restaurant, informed the hotel staff that a new amah was in the room, and enjoyed our first peaceful meal in about three weeks.

Of course we were taking a chance, but when a servant comes recommended and you get a good feeling about her as we did (which was especially reinforced when we returned from supper to find she had cleaned up our hotel suite without being asked), you can only hope for the best. Some people will never leave their children alone. They transfer all their own fears to them and only later wonder why their children are afraid to be left with a sitter.

You will hear occasional horror stories of child molestation by servants, but those stories are rare and usually there have been signs that something is going on long before it is actually discovered. I'm not recommending you throw all caution to the wind and hire just anyone, but it's like a lot of things overseas (medical care for instance): you simply have to go on faith that everything will turn out all right.

We'd all like to have a relative nearby, but that's next to impossible overseas, so unless you want to be trapped with your kids for the next few years, cross your fingers and hope for the best. And, rely on your own intuition about people. Besides, it's like hiring someone at home. If they don't work out, you give them notice and you dismiss them.

HOW TO INTERVIEW

If you're assigned to a foreign country which has a difficult language you know you'll never in a million years and countless survival courses be able to master, conduct the interview in English. If the person responds in anything remotely understandable to you, give him/her ten points. Language barriers, if your own skills are limited, can be a pain for three years unless you're a former world champ at charades.

In Beijing, where servants are assigned by a government bureau, interviews can rarely be conducted in English except through a translator. Subsequent communication, I discovered after hiring both cook and maid (known as ayi) can actually be carried out through facial expressions, raised eyebrows, and lots of pointing. It helps if your husband speaks the language.

Regardless of how you conduct the initial meeting – by yourself or with the help of an interpreter – it should be considered like any other potential employer-employee interview. You need to know expectations of hours, pay, responsibilities, holidays, and skills. And in return, you need to state your requirements. If you will be doing a lot of entertaining, you'll need someone with experience with large dinner parties or cocktail receptions. References help, but expatriate turnover often makes it difficult to follow them up. In the case of assigned personnel, like in Beijing, it is simply a matter of crossing your fingers and hoping for the best, which in China can mean hoping the government sends you a cook who really is a cook and not a driver pretending to be what you need that day.

The state of your servant's health can also be a critical issue to you, especially if you have young children or are planning a family. Don't be embarrassed to request that a maid have a thorough medical examination, most especially a chest X-Ray, to set your mind at ease. These days, it doesn't hurt to request an AIDs test as well if she is young and unmarried. In countries where houseboys are the common form of servant, I would definitely recommend all forms of testing. If they don't agree, don't hire them, unless they are balking due to financial considerations. In that case, if you have a good feeling about them but just want confirmation with tests, offer to pay. In Third World countries, medical tests are inexpensive by Western standards.

In many countries, your servants won't be limited to just maid or laundress. You could be hiring a driver, in which case your interview could take place on a test drive. After all, that is where his skills will be required, so why not check them out before you go ahead and hire a former kamikaze taxi driver. With a driver it also pays to ask him what expectations he may have for overtime. I've heard of stories where some drivers quit after just a few months because the couple rarely go out at night – lucrative hours for a full-time driver.

When hiring a cook, of course you must test him out at the kitchen and at the dinner table. Fortunately, bad cooks are uncovered after a few meals. Very often you have to demonstrate what you want done in the first few weeks.

LIVE-IN VERSUS PART-TIME

Often, this question is answered for you in countries where not only your servant will live in, but half her living relations as well. This is common in some developing countries, where your quarters may be a rambling villa with living space for many servants at the back of your house. I've known people who have never been quite sure just how many people they were actually supporting. In a Communist country like China, there is similarly no question about live-in status. They aren't even allowed to spend the night, never mind live with you. Chinese servants are stopped at the gates of the foreign compounds and checked regularly for their credentials.

Some apartments and homes come with so-called maid's quarters, but whoever designed many of them didn't have an able-bodied person in mind when considering space. We had a maid's room off our apartment in Bangkok that barely had air in it, but fortunately our maid returned to her own home every night and rarely stayed in it. We preferred that. When we lived in Taipei, the exorbitant price and lack of amah's quarters, limited us to part-time day help.

The amount of time you want your servant around will depend on a variety of factors, not the least of which will be your family configuration. With a new baby in a foreign country, you'll likely want available help 24 hours a day. Without children accompanying you, a part-time cleaning person or laundress will be all you require. It also depends on whether your help is in the country legally or not. For instance, when we lived in Taiwan, Filipina maids, many of them of the highest quality, were often working illegally and therefore had to be live-in or run the risk of an immigration round-up.

When you're living in a house, a full-time guard and gardener will also be a necessity. In general, these servants should be investigated as thoroughly as possible because many break-ins often do not involve a forced entry thanks to servants already working on the premises who know when madame and master are away on vacation or even out for the evening.

THE ABSENCE OF PRIVACY

Remember the point about a mixed blessing? With a houseful of servants, it will be difficult to ever feel alone in your own home. Someone will always be around, overhearing a conversation and walking in when they shouldn't. A friend of mine, a long-time resident of Bangkok, put it this way: to her, a day without servants will be the day she can use the bathroom and not have to close the door.

Your servants will know everything about you, including the number of times a week you make love with your husband. Don't ask me how they know, they do. In some countries, like China, the servants are expected to report on you and your family's activities regularly. In Thailand, my maid knew I was pregnant before my doctor confirmed it. You can't have your maid and privacy too, but you can certainly put up barriers for yourself. Close your bedroom door when you don't want to be disturbed during the day. It may seem like missy is taking a lot of naps, but you really are just creating a bit of space for yourself to quietly read a book or write a letter without feeling like somebody is watching. In socialist countries, it is simply a case of getting used to the fact that you are always likely under surveillance.

SPEAKING OF BARRIERS...

Most Westerners can't help it, but they want everyone to call them by their first name or indulge in other common acts of familiarity. I'm the worst offender, but I learned from experience that becoming overly familiar with people working for you in your own home can be hazardous to your mental health, to say nothing of your bank account.

It's hard not to treat someone living with you in your own home like family – especially if you are used to servants being part of the family – but please take my advice: on posting, keep your help at a distance emotionally. That's not to say you're not friendly and sensitive to their needs. It means keeping detached when sob story after sob story may come pouring out and somehow you get involved by either writing a cheque or doing their laundry.

HOW TO AVOID BEING CONTROLLED BY A SERVANT

When my daughter was born in Bangkok, I almost forgot she was truly my daughter and not a child born specifically for the pleasure of my Thai maid. I would return home from doing an errand to find about ten other Thai maids standing around my daughter's crib, paying homage to my maid for the perfect sleeping infant.

The worst incident by my reckoning was the day she grabbed a bottle of formula out of my hand claiming I was handling it wrong. Worse still, I ended that day with an attack of guilt because I made her cry when I went berserk.

Maybe I'm not the best person to be handing out advice on this subject, but I obviously acquired some newfound wisdom in my relationship with my Taiwanese amah. Perhaps she was just truly the gem I felt she was, because my husband (who dreads getting hysterical phone calls from me at his office, sobbing about the help) remarked while we were living there that for the first time in my life, I had help who wasn't trying to manipulate me.

I could still be nice and caring, but she would go home at the end of the day and I wouldn't take every sulk, sigh, or grunt personally. And neither should you, if you want to have a healthy relationship with your servant.

SERVANT LETHARGY

After three years in Thailand, my husband and I forgot how to fold clothes and put them away. It was easier to shove everything in the laundry basket so our maid could wash it before putting it away. Now admittedly, Bangkok weather rarely allowed anything to be worn twice, but even so, we would change our clothes constantly without thinking much about laundry. And then we returned home to Canada. After less than two weeks, I had eliminated everything made of cotton (which would require ironing) from our wardrobes and returned to perma press. We also re-learned the skill of picking up after ourselves, washing dishes, and preparing our own meals.

I've already mentioned the lethargy that comes from having a driver around – you forget how to walk. You also tend to forget that the closest you'll get back home to a chauffeur-driven ride is in a taxi. Try to remember that your true station in life is not the one you're enjoying as an expatriate overseas.

YOUR CHILDREN AND SERVANTS

As hard as I have found it, even with servants and nannies, I have always made it a point to make our bed every morning. My husband queried me about this at first, and my reply was instantaneous: I wanted our children to make their own beds and if they saw me being spoiled, how could I stop them from rebelling?

Never mind that a child can't make hospital corners too neatly, it is the effort that counts. The maid can re-make it, but I feel it's important to set an example. Sometimes it's hard to be a parent. If you want your children to grow up into spoiled brats turned adult, don't discipline them when they speak rudely to a servant. On the other hand, they can grow into nice people who know how to treat other people with respect if they learn early on how to show consideration to someone making their life abroad easier. Depending on age, some children will grow very attached to servants, usually enough to drive a mother into a jealous rage from time to time. It can't be helped and grinning and bearing it is the only solution, unless it's a case where the child never sees his parent and is reaching out for any affection offered. Consider that before going off on a tirade. Other mothers worry about attachments that will have to be eventually broken. On that point, there are several schools of thought and you have to decide which one you'll follow.

In my nuclear family – rotational foreign service – it would be difficult to ask all of us not to make attachments just because they will have to be broken in the not too distant future. We've followed the philosophy that says any attachment (and this applies to pets too) is worth having, even for a short time. We could live our whole lives giving up relationships just because they're not going to be too permanent. Nothing's permanent, and there's more to be gained from having loved a little than not at all. If a servant is good to your children, the relationship can't hurt and will be remembered fondly in the future.

SERVANTS AND DISCIPLINE

At the same time you want your children to respect your help and not bully them, you have to consider how you want your help to treat your children. The discipline issue usually involves lack of, rather than too much – you may have to physically restrain a maid or amah from spoiling your kid to death.

A servant is not a parent, and while you may want a maid to be as strict as possible and not let your child walk all over her, she also is not the one to hand out discipline. That's your job as a parent. One of the reasons I feel I've been lucky on both my postings, is that I ended up with help who were loving but firm with my children.

QUICK TIPS

Here is a list of useful things you need to know if you have servants while living overseas. Some of it may sound like simple common sense but you never know how easy it is to overlook such issues when you are starting out in a new country.

Tips and Tipping

Be sure you know what time of year your servant expects to be tipped. Chinese New Year or year's end, national holidays, religious holidays, even a birthday could be the time of year your servant, depending on the country, will receive a bonus or a cash present. Make sure you know the going rate, and how many of the servants around you (guards, etc.) also need to be tipped. Remember that if you stay for a few days with someone with servants, it is considered gauche not to tip them for helping make your visit pleasant (and likely doing your laundry). Be sure to ask your hostess what guidelines she may have set.

Insurance

Our Thai maid had her leg crushed under a motorcycle cab (a tuk tuk, the blight on Bangkok traffic) and while she wasn't working for us that day, we still felt responsible for her well-being. If she had been injured on the job, we would have been liable. Most insurance companies overseas offer something resembling a workmen's compensation policy, and it is worth having just in case.

Telephone Calls

One of the ways which confirmed I had a gem in my Taiwanese amah, was that she never once received or made a phone call while I was in the apartment. To me, that was a sign of a real professional (which she was). There is nothing more annoying than waiting for an urgent phone call yourself and taking messages for your maid, or trying to get your own line to check on your child and it's constantly engaged. Emergencies are one thing; idle chitchat with the amah next door is entirely another. Limit the use of the phone to emergencies only.

Outside Errands
I had a friend in Taipei who went positively nuts when she used to send her amah out for a loaf of bread and she would disappear for two hours, usually returning home without the bread. It's easier for you to do the outside work and let your maid stay put. The minute she goes out, you just know you'll be needed elsewhere.

Leaving Your Children Behind with Servants
It's tempting to travel when you're posted abroad, and let's face it, it's nice to have a break from your children. Depending on the age of your children, though, it can be a difficult decision to leave your children behind only with the servants. We were faced with this dilemma while living in Bangkok when we had an opportunity to travel down under to New Zealand. The solution we arrived at worked well, and we've used it again in future situations. We moved our baby – and Thai maid – into the house of good friends. Our friends didn't have to absorb the work of the baby because the maid was on hand, but we felt easier knowing our friends were there for emergencies. In our foreign community of friends, we all shared kids and maids from time to time so that parents could get a well-deserved break with peace of mind.

Servant Etiquette
Remember that the person you hire is helping you out, so try not to degenerate into a completely lazy person incapable of doing anything for yourself. They are doing enough for you, so heaping more upon them because you've forgotten how to do things for yourself isn't fair.

Cross-Cultural Sensitivity

When your servant sits down to a midday meal of what looks like glop, remember you are living in a foreign country where glop may be the national dish. Advise your children of their manners. What you eat may look like glop to them, too. Also take some of their superstitions and beliefs in stride and try to learn from them. When my daughter was born in Bangkok, my maid was firm in her belief that a stiff shot of scotch each evening would help shrink my uterus. Who was I to argue? When we traveled around the world on home leave, my Thai maid insisted on bringing food to the monks to bless our journey. I personally bought the rice.

FIRING YOUR MAID

It's never easy to fire a person from your employ, but if a servant is driving you so crazy that her help isn't worth the damage to your mental health, you should probably dismiss her from service. The standard rules of dismissal usually apply. That is, notice and compensation for at least two weeks' work.

The problem with firing maids overseas is that for some inexplicable reason, you may end up on a treadmill of hiring and firing. Many women will confirm this: either you hire a helper right from the start who then stays with you for the duration of your assignment; or you hire and fire someone on an average of once a month. I'm not suggesting you stick with someone who is truly unworkable, but often it's the case that the next one you hire won't be much better and the cycle will begin.

YOUR EXPECTATIONS OF
THE QUALITY OF SERVICE

Often this vicious cycle originates with your expectations of the quality of help a servant should provide. If you're a fastidious housekeeper, or the strictest of disciplinarians with your children, you run the risk of never being satisfied with the way your maid carries out her duties. You'll complain the house is not as clean and tidy as it should be; she can't cook to save her life; the sleeves of your blouses are not properly ironed; the flowers in the garden have grown too straggly and so on.

Don't expect to hire some absolutely perfect helper capable of reading your mind. When you like your house cleaned a certain way, you may have to show a servant how to do it your way. She may still be operating under her previous madame's agenda and doesn't know that you expect her to vacuum daily or clean out the fridge once a week. In the first place she may not even understand the way you speak.

In places like Beijing, where the standard of service is pretty low (with some exceptions) and the city is filthy from coal-burning braziers, there is no point trying to find some super-ayi to keep your apartment clean. And remember: if you were making a very minimum wage each day, chances are you wouldn't be busting your butt to make sure window ledges or every picture is dusted every day.

EXPLAINING ABOUT SERVANTS TO THE FAMILY BACK HOME

If you had servants during your stay abroad, get ready for the jokes: How's your slave? Tough life over there with all those servants? You will take a lot of teasing when you return home, either on leave or for good, about the fact that you had servants while living abroad. Your friends and family haven't got the faintest clue – unless they themselves have lived overseas – about the necessity of having help just to survive in an alien environment, so save your breath.

Your family will just assume that you are being spoiled silly and if the truth be told, you are. Enjoy the experience. It's definitely one of the bonuses of life abroad.

Chapter Seven

SOCIAL DIVERSIONS:
Making Friends and Entertaining Distractions

"...She gave the Minister of Guatemala a jeweled, emaciated hand to kiss; with a few smiling words made the banker's wife feel *passée*, provincial, and portly; flung an improper jest at the English lady whose embarrassment was mitigated by the knowledge that the wife of the French Military Attaché was *très bien née*; and drank three cocktails in rapid succession.

Dinner was served..."

—from the story 'Dinner Parties'
by Somerset Maugham (1922)

Colonialism and imperial style entertainments may have gone the way of the British Raj, but the rigid social 'niceties' and petty social circuits which were literary fodder for Maugham and other travel writers of his era are still, unfortunately, followed to the letter in many foreign communities. In other words, I am not entirely convinced that Maugham's descriptive dinner party cannot be found playing out somewhere in the world today. I know, because I've seen such ridiculous social tableaux played out before my egalitarian eyes.

"And what is your husband's position in the embassy?" a newly-arrived diplomatic wife may be asked while she frantically balances teacup and a slice of some freshly baked specialty of her hostess's cook.

"He's a second secretary in the foreign aid section," may be the response from a woman uninitiated into the intricate business of social stratification.

"Oh." The response is curt but always polite, cutting the new wife dead before she can even wipe the crumbs from her lips. It is delivered completely deadpan, with eyes glazed over by a total lack of social interest. The person posing the question then moves on to the next – hopefully higher ranked – new face at the coffee morning.

This is not to say that members of business communities overseas cannot be equally as guilty as diplomats in clinging to ludicrous and anachronistic pecking orders as if they were lifelines. Based on my own bias (against), or just from my own jaded experience where I've seen with my own eyes the scene I just described, overseas bureaucrats often seem more obvious and odious in their pretentious displays of self-importance. My patience runs thin with those diplomatic wives who forget they revert back to ordinary mortals the moment their plane lands back in their own country.

Whenever I complain about these snobs and their social behavior based on completely inflated convictions of position and influence, my foreign service husband is quick to remind me that diplomats achieve their sense of well-being from order, and particularly social order when abroad. Business people, he will point out, have routes other than social snobbery open to them for achieving personal satisfaction. They can go off and count their money.

MISUNDERSTANDING THE PECKING ORDER

When you are new to international life, you may wonder how expatriates can possibly tolerate living in foreign communities which adhere to completely intangible class structures. The unfortunate answer is that many expatriates always have and will continue to live by these arbitrary social conventions. It forms the basis of their overseas lives. Without them, they would be lost.

A true story: When my husband was a third secretary in Bangkok, we were accidentally invited to a reception hosted by the Prime Minister in honor of the King's birthday. I say 'accidentally' because the invitation was not addressed to the diplomat in the family, but to the journalist – myself.

Most of the foreign press corps in Bangkok were old hands at this particular annual event, and gave it a pass. Not us. We were still new to Bangkok, thought it would be a lark, and so, going against my own rule (which is to skip all diplomatic parties unless I know the food is going to be good) I suggested we attend. My husband foolishly went along with the idea.

We decided to allow an embassy car and driver to transport us to the affair instead of chauffeuring ourselves as we normally did in our beat-up, ten-year-old Mazda (with western Canadian frost shields plastered to the windows, and block heater plugs dangling out the front). This was fortunate for us, because when approaching the venue – a tremendously pillared, sweeping front drive, palace-style building – we found ourselves in a line-up of Mercedes, carrying bored-looking bejeweled guests waiting to be discharged at the front door.

At the next queue, this one made up of people and not livery, we ran into our own Canadian Ambassador and his wife who looked surprised to see us in the reception line. In a quick exchange of pleasantries, we discovered the invitations had been issued to only the top and number two diplomats of each mission. I started to sweat in my Thai silk.

"Let's bolt," I pleaded with my husband only moments before shaking the Prime Minister's hand.

Negative. "Are you out of your mind?" Followed by a stage whisper likely designed to exonerate him from responsibility for our gaffe: "You're the journalist. You're the one who suggested we come in the first place."

Luckily for us, our Ambassador was a wonderful egalitarian type and made the necessary introductions seem painless as we all carried on into the palace.

That was the last anybody spoke with us. Diplomatic niceties were in full swing. We were nobodies, unworthy of conversation. We wandered around aimlessly until we figured out we were a lowly-ranked island unto ourselves. We had to be mature about this, we assured each other. Naturally, we started to giggle and couldn't stop. Seizing the precise moment we could politely leave, I finally got my wish to bolt. The only balm to our egos was a glimpse of the Nepalese Ambassador. In full national dress, which included a pink scarf around his head, he also wandered around in a daze. Apparently he didn't know anybody either.

SOCIALIZING WHEN YOU FIRST ARRIVE

Even the most experienced expatriates will tell you that it's not easy to feel socially at ease when you are part of a newly-arrived couple at a posting abroad. You are blank slates, individually and as a couple, and those people you come into contact with will invariably wait to see how the slate is filled in before making any moves.

Your husband's job is the first and primary criteria on which you are judged, especially the rank which his job carries, whether it be diplomatic or financial, academic or military. As a mere wife, you are simply Mrs. Husband's Job, and any initial social interchange will stem from that fact. Sad, but true.

On first glance, you are who you are married to. People will slot you – and either proceed or stop dead in their tracks – based on that most dreaded of all questions, some variation on the scenario I have described which always comes down to this: "And what does your husband do?"

Until you get your social bearings and shake your initial feelings of culture shock which can also bring with it complete social disorientation, these discriminatory and subjective social judgments will seem like yet another hardship to endure, along with hot weather or language barriers. They should be treated the same though, because eventually, not unlike the other shocks of a new culture, you will become accustomed to them and adjust your life accordingly.

By the way, not all foreign communities are necessarily rigid, but there's a hint of these misnamed social 'graces' everywhere. On our posting to Taiwan, where the diplomatic community is sparse due to Taiwan's international standing, the first thing I noticed was the absence of social protocol. I immediately attributed the more relaxed atmosphere to the limited number of diplomats. When I pointed this out to various corporate wives, I was informed that social ranking did indeed exist. Among various larger multinational corporations, where the expatriate positions numbered more than half a dozen, there was in fact a pecking order, as petty as the best of them.

And there were other instances of social ranking in Taipei: in cases where an expatriate husband was heavily involved in deal making, the couple kept most of their night-time entertainment limited to people who could advance business ventures. The nurturing of new friendships was not as important a goal as the pursuit of money.

We were lucky in Taipei: as my husband was a mere language student at the time, we were completely off the social scale, irrelevant politically and out of touch economically. These factors had the surprising effect of liberating us totally and we actually enjoyed a year of intense partying with people who sought us out for mere friendship, as opposed to the useful contact in what I call 'counterpart' friendships. Sometimes it is more fun to be ordinary mortals overseas.

On the other hand, it is never fun to be on the receiving end of someone else's racial prejudices. Families who move from the developing Third World to Western countries may at some point face this issue, even if it comes strictly in some benign form of racial ignorance. (A Taiwanese friend who moved to Canada said she was often mistaken in shopping malls for a native Canadian Indian.) Unfortunately, there is no sure-fire piece of advice to offer here on how to deal with prejudice other than the general theme I've been threading throughout this book: be true to yourself and about yourself. Self-confidence goes a long way towards silencing verbal barrages of prejudice. And be sure to watch out for signs that your children are not also on the receiving end of it and unable to cope. They may not have the emotional maturity to dismiss prejudice and will need your help as a mother to explain why it exists.

INSECURITY IN THE EARLY DAYS

Why are people snobs? If taken to mean socializing only with known quantities instead of the pretentious petty behavior I have mentioned earlier, snobbery makes people feel safe inside a warm and secure social cocoon. A person enters a room and knows everybody there, everybody knows them, and the party begins.

As a newly-arrived wife, you will feel desperately unsure of yourself and your ability to ever break into that cocoon – that is, the various social cliques. In the early days it can be tough to gain admittance and not only because of who your husband is, but because nobody knows what kind of person you are yet. Expatriates are often accused of engaging in instant friendships but even by accelerated expatriate time frames, don't expect to have instant friends within mere days of your arrival. It takes a few get-togethers to have even the slightest history of shared good times on which to form the basis of a friendship. In other words, don't instantly dismiss your powers of making new friends and get even more desperately insecure about yourself, on the basis of a twenty-minute chat over coffee which you feel led nowhere. Remember that those close friends back home have been friends for years, not mere minutes. And bear in mind your frame of mind: as a jet-lagged, culture shocked, stressed out mother of young children trapped in a hotel room for eight hours without help, it's not that easy to make a good impression.

By the way, those insecure feelings can be even further compounded if a husband and wife are not just newcomers to a certain country, but to expatriate life itself. They may find themselves standing around listening to conversations about far-flung places they can barely pinpoint on the map. Everyone, it will seem, has lived hither and yonder, or traveled there (airplane stories are very popular at expatriate functions) and will feel overwhelmed by an inability to contribute to the conversation.

Experience has to be earned, there is no way around that, but eventually you too will have stories to share. In the meantime, remember that every storyteller needs a good audience, so play that role to the hilt. And read, read, read. Be current about the affairs of your host culture. The market for travel books – not guides, but true literary collections and journals – has also exploded in the last ten years. The material is just out there, waiting for you to read. And don't worry. It doesn't take long to fit in. Your first home leave or trip in the region will give you a few of your own traveler's tales.

PROTOCOL: OFFICIAL AND JUST PLAIN MEAN

What is protocol? My dictionary offers a reasonable definition which can easily apply to overseas life: 'a code of diplomatic or military etiquette and precedence.'

The reason I like my dictionary's meaning is that while it stresses etiquette (which I will address eventually, I promise) it also mentions the idea of precedence. I have lived my entire life fleeing from conformity. I suppose that makes me a protocol basher, but it's my opinion that everyone needs an escape valve when living overseas and breaking from protocol is so far not punishable by death.

As a wife, it is possible to break from protocol in some instances without destroying your husband's career. Do not let him convince you otherwise. You need to be able to escape from suffocating social rules overseas because so many of them were made in the last century and should be stuffed away in a trunk along with white gloves and hats. Life is suffocating enough in a small foreign community without your own culture imposing rigid rules of behavior which have no relation to modern woman.

For instance, I like to make friendships on the basis of mutual empathy and interests: not because a woman is the wife of my husband's counterpart at some other mission and my husband wants us all to be friends. I equally despise the tyrannical rules which dictate that I be standing by my husband's side at every cocktail party, dinner party or social event of the hour. If these soirées happen to fall during the dinner hour, in a city which requires my spending an hour or more in bumper to bumper traffic, to arrive hot and sweaty for a function which may last another twenty-five minutes after I finally get there...well, forget it is what I say. I'm not going, regardless of who the event is being held for. It's my husband's role to go to official functions. I have other things to do, like my own work, or putting my children to bed.

The rule which says my presence is required was written long before expatriate women pursued meaningful work of their own while abroad, and at a time when servants became surrogate parents. If a woman really is interested in going, that's another matter but nobody should be forced. If a woman's absence reflects badly on her husband, we're back to the 1950's again.

By the same token, however, stuffy, male chauvinistic protocol should not exclude women from social events if they're interested in getting out for the evening. This happens in one or two ways. There are some cultures which simply don't include women in night-time entertainment. The Japanese are a prime example. Women are virtually shut out of the night life.

Respecting another culture – even the most extreme male chauvinism – more or less goes with the territory. It's easier to understand, though, when it's a foreign culture excluding women. But in some instances, it is her own husband who is shutting her out. Too many times, a husband will dismiss the wife from an event with the words: "It's only for the office staff" and then proceed to stay out long after midnight while the wife twiddles her thumbs back home wondering where he is. And with whom. (More on this subject in chapter nine.)

Expatriate wives are too often the hapless social victims of protocol, real or contrived, while their husbands in a very typical overseas situation seem to have the best of all possible worlds. The men are better equipped to deal with many of the arbitrary rules of foreign society because ultimately their work will help them to block out any ruthless inequities and get on with their lives. Protocol may be a pain for the man sometimes, but it just doesn't get in his way on a daily basis. He can too often use it to his advantage.

The wife, meanwhile, not only often feels left out by her own husband, but she can also be literally stuck in neutral, her wheels spinning because protocol – and this is where the petty, subjective, pretentious form of protocol usually comes in – has slammed other doors in her face, stopped friendships which may otherwise have blossomed, and destroyed her self-confidence to the point she is convinced it must be her breath or something else which has stopped people from phoning her up. By the time she realizes it's just narrow-minded social inequities or worse, a philandering husband, she may have become a complete emotional zombie. Or returned home, shattered.

One final word on snobbery for now: there are snobs everywhere, even at home. There are also social rules at home and not just in these overseas settings. Remember that in a small overseas community, snobbery will seem more annoying and interfering because your community has shrunk, and your self-esteem may be at an all-time low from the other adjustments you are making.

So follow the path of common sense. Get on with your life the best way you know how and make your own efforts at friendship. Learn to ignore the people who place too much emphasis on intangibles. Trust your own instincts about the people you do want to get to know better. It is possible to lead a satisfying life without getting all caught up in social orders, but success will definitely depend on your own attitude. And if it is the case that it is your own husband who carries rank, ignore the inevitable obsequious sycophants.

THE JERK THEORY

This is a good point to introduce my own theory of social intercourse abroad because sometimes you may wrongly – and too quickly – dismiss a potential friend as a jerk, a nobody, a wimp, or any other words you may want to use to describe someone you don't intend to pay further attention to.

My theory usually plays out this way: You're at a cocktail party or dinner party and you're introduced to someone (it can be a man or woman). The person who brought you together is called away to another conversation and you're left making small talk with this new face. The other person may be (a) sweating like crazy; (b) drunk as a skunk; (c) talking too much or too loudly; (d) constantly dropping things like a napkin or plate of hors d'oeuvre; (e) experiencing rapid eye movement around the room to the exclusion of your own face.

What a jerk, you think, and plot how to get away as quickly as possible. The first impression has been bad, and were you at home, you would likely avoid setting eyes on the person again.

But in a small overseas foreign community, you probably will meet again. And on the second meeting, you may discover the following facts: (a) the night you met, the person was newly-arrived and had brought all the wrong clothing. His/her lightweight clothing was still too heavy for the warm climate and he/she finally had just finally found the time to buy some clothes which put a stop to the constant sweating which was getting downright embarrassing; (b) the last time you met, it's explained, the person had not had a chance to eat anything all day because of a bad stomach bug and had foolishly downed a drink too quickly and had got positively snapped; hence (c) he/she found herself babbling like crazy at a drunkenly high pitch and (d) dropping everything in sight. Finally (e) the person who had brought him/her (not the introducer) and was supposed to take him/her home had seemingly vanished from the party and no matter where he/she frantically looked, the person was not to be found. It turns out a wild taxi cab ride back home had put the capper on that particular evening.

You find this person as entertaining as can be while confessing this litany of culture shocked woe, and you think how fortunate it was to have run into each other again because your first impression was most definitely wrong.

You have learned a valuable lesson: overseas, the benefit of the doubt should be exercised beyond the normal boundaries of home. People are uptight when they have moved to a foreign country. First impressions are very often negative because the person was uncomfortable for a variety of reasons. Remember that you probably appeared in a similar unflattering light your first few months. Give everyone a chance. You may make a good friend that way. On the other hand: if on the subsequent two or three meetings, the person does not seem to improve, really is a jerk in fact, then keep your distance.

WHAT TO WEAR:
DRESS NOT TO BE DEPRESSED

I've always been a self-conscious person about clothes, preferring to dress for myself and saying to hell with everyone else even while fretting miserably about it. When we were posted briefly to New York City, I could barely force myself out the apartment/hotel door if I didn't feel I could blend in with the well-dressed and definitely more well-heeled humanity on the sidewalks below. If you are a person whose indecisiveness causes her to rip apart her closet before social events, day outings, even just to hang around the house, be careful: when you are making a cultural transition to a new country, often with dramatic changes in climate, the contents of your wardrobe can have an equally dramatic effect on the state of your mind.

Not only will you be dealing with the sartorial styles and codes of the host culture, but the way in which the expatriate culture dresses may also contribute to your angst, especially at social functions. You don't necessarily want to stand out – or worse yet, be singled out for a major gaffe – but how were you to know the rest of the wives took 'informal' to mean dresses and stockings when back home the same dress code meant sweat suits?

Dress up rather than down in the early days for parties. Often, the venue will also help you select your clothes. Receptions held at hotels or other public places are usually fancier than at-home parties. Take note of social customs as well. For example, in Muslim countries, short, tight skirts are frowned upon, especially at official functions and other ceremonies where religion is involved.

ATTENDING A DINNER PARTY VERSUS COCKTAIL PARTY

Most people have a preference and I advise women to pick theirs if they intend to try to limit their attendance at official entertainments. Personally, as a guest, I tend to choose the dinner party, especially the sit-down variety. My reason is simple: at a dinner party you can actually have a conversation with someone because people can't walk around eating a full course meal. It's a stationary event, at least the dinner portion of it. Because I have designated my preference, I tend to go almost exclusively to dinner parties when I can't possibly get out of attending an official/diplomatic function.

Mind you, being seated (trapped by a table) does have its own drawbacks. I was once trapped between an empty chair and the guest of honor at a dinner party hosted by the

Apostolic Pronuncio in Bangkok. On my left was a high-ranking Canadian Cardinal, known for his amazing endeavors in support of the poor in Africa and Asia. He wasn't my problem. On the contrary, we had spent an enjoyable afternoon at a Thai orphanage where I had the privilege of interviewing this eighty-year-old priest after he had enchanted the orphans by riding on an elephant. I was delighted to have the opportunity to speak to him some more. But seated on his left was an elderly Canadian nun, a long-standing resident of Thailand, who was not about to be upstaged by this babbling Jewish girl who in her view had been mistakenly seated next to this important Catholic personage. I could hear her mind ticking over: What was the Pronuncio thinking by seating her there?

As for cocktail receptions, the reason I choose to avoid going to them is because I feel they tend to be flighty affairs. People perch on each other, like birds, for mere seconds before spotting another prey and flying off. The conversations, which only last mere seconds, are typically pointless and often surreal. In my view, cocktail parties are too short given the time commitment. You always end up all dressed up with nowhere to go after one. You also eat too much and spoil your dinner with greasy hors d'oeuvre. Spring rolls, if you're stationed in the Far East, are the worst offenders.

HOSTING PARTIES

As a hostess, my preference is reversed: I would rather give a cocktail reception any day over a sit-down dinner for twelve, unless it's twelve close friends.

As a hostess, with a thousand and one things on your mind, the distraction factor is too high to be able to concentrate on any worthwhile conversation. Therefore, a cocktail party is ideal. You can constantly excuse yourself and head off to confer with the hired help who are actually doing all the work for the evening. At your own dinner party, you have to be polite and smile a lot at some visiting widget salesman or politician (the latter tend to be easier, mind you, because they see everyone as a potential voter and treat everyone with equal friendliness).

Before we leave the subject of parties altogether, here are a few of my own serious – and a few irreverent – tips on etiquette for giving and surviving them:

(1) Be aware of the cultural or religious persuasions of your guests, especially if you're living in a Muslim country where alcohol and pork are taboo; for Hindus, beef is forbidden.

(2) If you have to give a lot of dinner parties, experienced hostesses recommend you keep a record of what food and wine you served to whom on what date so you don't repeat yourself (some women like to keep track of what they wore as well).

(3) Make sure you have enough help if it's your party. In most foreign communities, there are freelance waiters who work nights helping the expatriates entertain each other.

(4) Women with tendencies toward heated debate (on subjects like feminism especially) should make every effort to restrict themselves to bland conversation and small talk at expatriate social functions which are devoid of any substance for the women participants: learn to speak only about what you have recently purchased at some ridiculously small sum.

(5) Eat before you go to either dinner or cocktail party, for overseas the former tends to begin late and the latter offers few distractions other than hors d'oeuvre. This technique also helps stop you from implanting yourself in front of the food table.

(6) As a hostess, never invite anyone far above your own social ranking, for this can lead to a very dull – and quiet – party if the guests feel there is no one there they can speak to, especially the host and hostess.

(7) Decide if you plan to be an air kisser or not. I find it ridiculous to kiss people I've met only once or twice, but air kissing is rampant on the expatriate circuit and a consistent position should be adopted before heading out into the social

whirl. At the same time, remember the social etiquette of other countries which may, for instance, forbid any physical contact (including shaking hands) between members of the opposite sex unless they are blood relations.

OTHER DISTRACTIONS

Life overseas is not just one long cocktail party. There are other frivolous amusements which can distract the expatriate wife who chooses not to seek employment, not to study language, or not to take any highbrow cultural courses. I'd like to say at the outset that while this discussion will likely be viewed as tongue in cheek – and in part it is meant to make fun of myself and others like me – I've engaged in every last one of them at one time or another.

Going to the Hairdresser

The BBC, known for its bizarre documentaries on everything from rare wildlife to outer space, once explored in detail the life of another offbeat species, namely the expatriate wife. In this particular documentary, the wives in question lived in Hong Kong. I am singling out this program because during the interviews, one of the Hong Kong expatriate wives made a comment that is relevant to this discussion of life overseas. She said, "There is no excuse for a woman not to be well-groomed in Hong Kong." I laughed so hard I thought my husband's British cousins, with whom I was watching the program, were going to think there was something wrong with me. I couldn't possibly explain to them well enough that the comment was simply perfect.

Going to the hairdresser is one of the most common distractions for expatriate wives. I happen to enjoy washing my own short curly hair in the shower and rarely have time for anything but a botched home manicure, but there is absolutely no need for one to engage in this manual labor on some postings, and many women don't. Perfect hair, nails and toes can be seen as part of the uniform of an expatriate wife. Hanging out in beauty parlors can take up a good part of the morning and certainly kill the time before meeting someone for lunch.

Tennis

This is another popular pastime of the expatriate wife, along with golf where available. Most expatriate clubs in foreign settings will offer various leagues and tournaments which can essentially allow women to play every day if they wish. If you decide to play in any expatriate wives' league, make sure you're good at it. There are some women who rarely play for 'fun.' These are the women who have channeled so much of their frustrated creative energy into tennis, that a simple match can become a very serious proposition.

Shopping

There can be no end to shopping bonanzas for the overseas wife, for in addition to shops with easy local access, most international women's clubs arrange for a variety of day excursions to other shopping opportunities which may not be easy to reach on your own. I don't have any personal experience with these excursions (my own shopping style is limited to complete blow-outs in bookstores around the world although I have been known to have a complete personality change when presented with the consumer smorgasbord in Hong Kong) but I've been told that bargains and exotica abound on these day trips.

Shopping tours are also arranged within various regions. This is certainly the case within the Asian sphere where expatriate wives fly off in groups of half a dozen or more to major shopping capitals in Korea, Hong Kong, Singapore, and Thailand. I'm told that these junkets provide a perfect outlet for women who like to 'shop till they drop' because cultural sights are normally not included on these tours in order to maximize spending time.

Bitch and Stitch Luncheon Groups
There are variations on this theme everywhere but its essence should be obvious. Women gather to complain about maids, husbands and overseas life generally while sewing, viewing a fashion show, learning how to arrange flowers and other wifely activities.

Having a Baby
This option is limited to certain age groups, but from personal experience this is a wonderful way to distract you during your overseas posting. There are medical appointments, prenatal classes, city-wide searches for baby things and lots of guilt-free napping and eating associated with this activity. After the birth, there are exercise classes and playgroups to fill your day.

Entertaining Visitors from Home
This activity is usually accompanied by high levels of stress, depending on where you are posted in the world. If you have adequate help and the city is not completely

chaotic, you will have an easier time of it because your guests will be inclined to venture out by themselves. Otherwise, you can end up with guests who prefer to never leave your home, even after it's pointed out to them that they have traveled thousands of miles to virtually be prisoners in an apartment or house.

Part of the problem of entertaining friends and family from home is that depending on the distance they've traveled, they feel obliged to stay for at least a month.

Try to limit your hospitality to two weeks maximum or silent screaming will become your new pastime. Also attempt to set ground rules before arrival such as: guests are required to spend a certain number of hours on their own each day in order for the hostess to recover her cool. If it's a mother-in-law coming to visit, absolutely insist that your husband take time off before letting her in the door. Plan these visits well ahead of time, and where possible, do advance work on all excursion destinations. Try to avoid arriving anywhere sight unseen, especially with parents.

MAKING FRIENDS

I'll try to be more serious now, because making friends overseas is serious business. Ask a woman how she survived a difficult posting (ask me about Taiwan for instance) and she will more often than not tell you it was because of some wonderful friend who pulled her through. Sure, activities and projects and clubs all provide distractions, but we all need soul mates, someone with whom we share complete empathy.

In a foreign environment, where many things are unfamiliar, a best friend can be like a security blanket to be dragged around with you. If you're not together, you're checking in with one another to compare that day's horror stories or achievements. It's your point of contact with a new order of living.

Many of these friendships will seem to happen by sheer serendipity, but mutual interests or stage of life is usually a powerful incentive. While some initial factor may spark acquaintance, many shared interests are usually learned in those incredible first conversations of discovery.

I had only been living in Bangkok long enough to confirm I was pregnant with my first child when I started a Thai language class for expatriate wives. Sitting in a row along an open window (the school had an open-air concept, allowing the clatter of geese and chickens from a courtyard below to effectively shut out the teachers' voices), about eight of us dependents sat fanning ourselves, myself especially since the early days of pregnancy were not my most comfortable. We were learning the Thai words for our various nationalities. When a woman down the row said she was from Canada, followed by my own declaration only moments later, we both quietly leaned forward to get a better look at the other fellow countrywoman. Later, after class, we naturally sought each other out, only to discover we were about two weeks apart in our pregnant states – both for the first time – and the friendship blossomed from there. I simply could not have survived without her and other soul mates I was lucky enough to connect with in Taipei and Beijing.

There are lots of ways besides women's meetings to make new friends. One absolutely foolproof way is through the international schools, but this naturally will only hold true for women traveling with children. Home and school associations have a highly trained radar for seeking out volunteers for absolutely everything and will likely contact you before your last box is unpacked. You don't need to go the official route either to make friends through the school. Simply ask your son or daughter who they may wish to play with after school, and presto, you're on the phone to another woman.

Language classes, mothers' groups, health clubs, or supermarket checkouts can all be scouted for new friends: if you are pro-active in reaching out. You won't necessarily like everyone you meet, but foreign communities offer few shortages of people to try out, bearing in mind all the social 'niceties' I mentioned earlier. Where there are no built-in communities offered by corporate families or embassies, remember that you will have to muster your own self-confidence to phone up people and arrange meetings. No one can do this for you.

Your local neighbors as well as the wives of your husband's local colleagues are valuable friends to have. You can meet local people in other situations too such as at work, at ante-natal classes, in church, in local choirs, at health clubs, in public libraries...the possibilities are endless. What is important is the willingness to overcome that 'local/expatriate' barrier which unfortunately often includes a subconscious racial barrier. Sad but true. Initially, exchanges are brief and sometimes awkward but eventually there will come a moment when you can suggest a cup of coffee together or lunch and a wonderful friendship blossoms.

SHAKING FRIENDS

We are all eager to please when we first move somewhere new, and in our eagerness we sometimes tend to reach out and touch virtually everyone in our naiveté. Unfortunately, we sometimes embrace friendships which we quickly discover are not meant to be. The dilemma then arises: how to escape a bad situation in a small community? The chance of not bumping into a person again is pretty slim.

Friendships which stop cold because of lack of kindred spirit – as opposed to lack of social standing or due to a major disagreement – are bound to happen overseas just as they might happen at home. You may begin a friendship with the best of intentions, but conversation quickly fades to nothing, or you discover you simply can't stand the way her kids treat yours. There are a thousand and one reasons.

Be polite about it if you run into one of those never-to-be friends. If you feel like it was going nowhere, there's a good chance she may have been thinking the same thing about you and was equally worried about how to extricate herself from an uncomfortable situation. Not every friendship which starts out easily will necessarily blossom. So when you see each other, make appropriate small talk but don't lie to each other about plans which will never be carried out. See this as a golden opportunity to get off the phoney 'let's have lunch' treadmill.

Friendships which wither after a major argument or falling out can be more problematic in small communities. Try hard not to bring other people into your fight. It makes everyone uncomfortable. If you must make more of an effort to meet people overseas, by the same token you have to be more willing to rise above petty squabbles overseas. Agree to disagree and get on with your lives. A posting is too short to carry grudges.

LOSING FRIENDS

We say goodbye a lot during an expatriate life. People are constantly moving on, including yourself, and sometimes it seems like you were just getting to know someone when confirmation for their next posting comes through.

There's no way around this fact of life, but there are a few ways some women try to protect their emotions, not all of which I necessarily agree with.

Many women I know – especially ones who are permanent expatriates who stay in places longer than rotational people – prefer to make friends only with others whom they know will be around for a while, at least two years. This certainly helps you avoid becoming attached to someone whose local shelf life is limited, but at the same time, you never know what a brief friendship may hold.

Recognize that you will have to say goodbye eventually and then enjoy the days together with someone whose company and opinions you enjoy. Those capricious social codes are often unavoidable, but choosing new friends on the basis of time constraints is your own doing and can be avoided. It seems to be harder when your friends leave the post rather than vice versa, because when you are on the move, the distractions are enormous and it's hard to focus on anything but what is at hand. When a friend pulls up and leaves a hole in your daily routine, however, you will feel at a loss and slightly disoriented to be sure.

We returned to Taipei from a European holiday just after my closest friend, a Taiwanese/Canadian woman, had moved to the United States. For the first few days we were back, I thought it was jet lag which was making me feel so fuzzy and unfocused. And then it hit me: my friend was gone and I had to readjust my time accordingly. As I wrote in a letter to her shortly after she left: suddenly I could work without distractions and it was killing me. I missed her a lot.

It sounds trite when put into words, but even though you are saying goodbye to close friends, you probably will see them again if you make the effort to keep in touch by mail and phone. Organize reunions wherever possible. Any friendship, even brief ones or those carried out across twelve time zones, are worth having and remembering. It's a benefit of life abroad which can't be written into a contract.

Chapter Eight

HOME LEAVE
It May Not Be To Heaven

I did some creative editing of Webster's words (I know a thing or two about taking words out of context as I used to be a television reporter) and came up with an intriguing definition for home leave which isn't too far from the reality. Home leave, given selective meanings, can be when the social unit formed by persons living together in exile, having received authorized permission to be absent from duty, departs for a congenial environment in its place of origin.

But let's forget about the dictionary, particularly that part about 'a congenial environment in its place of origin.' If that's supposed to mean the home of a loving family member, happy to see you all after a year or more of guilt-ridden letters of professed homesickness, with doors thrown open to you and no emotional strings attached, then the tooth fairy *does* exist.

Yes, you can go home again, and even have a good time. But this doesn't happen by divine right. It requires proper planning and adopting realistic expectations.

WHAT MAKES HOME LEAVE SUCH A TOUCHY SUBJECT?

This is not a riddle. What do you call two people who can't stop talking, fighting, eating, packing, flying, driving, packing, eating, drinking, fighting, shopping, spending, drinking, eating etc., etc.? Answer: an expatriate couple who has just spent a fortune to be pampered/tortured by family on an annual home leave.

And so it follows, what do you call a person doing all of the items listed above, by herself, with several children in tow, surrounded by in-laws who drive her crazy, and immediate family which may not offer an ounce of sympathy or help because they are too resentful and/or just plain uninterested in her overseas life? Answer: an expatriate wife on home leave, of course!

Old hands at the game know there are three subjects over which expatriate couples can be relied upon to engage in heated argument. The first two – sex and money – don't count since you don't need to live overseas to fight about those time-honored themes of marital discord.

Home leave, on the other hand, is never a subject which can just lie there. It is fraught with danger, debate, and emotional disaster.

WHERE TO STAY

Depending on your entitlement and company or government benefits, the subject of home leave will normally come up about halfway through the first year abroad. It's often triggered by thoughts about family, or your old neighborhood, or something which sets off a bout of homesickness.

It may also come after a conversation with another wife who has informed you that the foreign community completely bolts once the international school closes for the summer. You discover that there will be nobody for you or your children to do things with, and seasonal temperatures will be high enough to induce comas. The danger begins when you begin to consider where you will stay during your home leave.

"We have to go home this summer," you'll tell your husband, idealizing family members who actually annoy you, and rhapsodizing over shops or streets which normally you ignore. "OK," he'll say. "But I don't want to stay with your parents for longer than a week, so we'll take a holiday somewhere before visiting my parents on the way back."

"A week?!" you'll cry. "That's not enough time! They still haven't forgiven me for taking the grandchildren out of the country. Are you crazy? I can't go home for just a week! We'll have to stay for at least two weeks, minimum."

Flash forward.

"Why did you listen to me," you cry to your husband in the privacy of the 'spare' bedroom being used as your home leave command post.

The excess baggage is piled high to the ceiling; laundry (which you may not have done personally in at least a year) litters the floor while you secretly try to throw out your husband's shirts which need ironing; five bags of new unopened tubes of the only toothpaste your children will brush with, and twenty-four 100 per cent cotton panties have been thrown carelessly on the bed after that day's five-minute reprieve, alone, in the local mall.

You turn to your husband and unburden all of it: "My mother is driving me crazy, nobody will let me sleep off my jet lag, and I'm already eating too much!!"

You've been home three days.

Second scenario: Your brother or sister fervently insisted on the availability of space in their new house which could cozily accommodate all of you, even with their own children and pets and possibly other sleeping-over friends or relatives. It's summer, they laugh, when the living is easy. Throw another steak on the barby.

That's a common idealized fantasy of a sibling relationship which may be playing on some parallel dimensional planet, but not here on Earth. Think about it: if you fought like cats and dogs when you were younger and there were no wives, husbands, children, or in-laws, how can you possibly believe you won't get on each other's nerves when you and your family arrive jet-lagged and culture shocked, dragging enough luggage for an army of home leavers?

WHO SHOULD YOU VISIT?

Here's another threatening area: trying to figure out in advance which people you will allot precious, limited time to see. It is a maxim of the unwritten rules governing home leave: every known relative – and ones so distant you only remember hearing their name once, possibly mentioned by your ageing grandmother – will want a piece of you when you arrive home from overseas.

So will all your friends.

But here's the catch. Everyone wants to see you, but nobody wants to hear you. Let me set the scene once again. You walk through the door and embrace your sister/oldest girlfriend/maybe even your mother.

"It's so good to see you!!" you overlap each other, not unlike the preceding year of long distance telephone calls down that time-delayed international voice wind tunnel. "Tell me everything!!!" your mother/sister/girlfriend manages to edge out over you.

"Well…" you begin breathlessly. "We're living on the most amazing street, filled with these people who…"

"Do you like my hair?" they interrupt within ten seconds. "There's a new hair styler at your old beauty salon and you wouldn't believe what a mess they made of so-and-so's hair…"

"Is that right?" you reply, your mind – and mouth – braking to a halt. Then, quickly getting a handle on the situation, you ask, "How is so-and-so?"

"Well…" they begin breathlessly. And you eat the cake/sandwich/bun/caloric whatsit already placed before you.

Another twisted Murphy's Law of home leave: you never get to spend more than thirty seconds with the friends you really want to see. Fortunately, they will understand the most and continue to write long letters when you return abroad.

And then there's the relative or friend of a friend you have to visit who knows the country you're living in better than you do, despite the fact that they've never been there.

"I was reading an article about that place you're posted to the other day," some know-it-all will pontificate at you.

Depending on the state of your jet lag, or the stage of your leave (tolerance levels run higher at the beginning due to excitement), you will either respond politely or ram the piece of cake you're once again eating down somebody's throat.

You smile a lot on your round of home leave courtesy calls. You develop set pieces as well. On automatic talking pilot, you will be able to give an abridged version or the documentary length discourse on your life overseas without actually thinking. Old hands can plan the next visit on their agenda while seemingly gush about the new culture they're learning about.

Nobody wants to hear anything negative. After all, they figure you have an army of servants peeling you grapes all day. Dare to mention the air virus your son picked up because the local children use the street as a toilet and the comment back to you will be: "So why don't you come home?"

"Maybe because my husband's job is over there and I want my marriage to continue," you mutter, very very quietly. Smile and eat your cake.

THE HIGH PRICE OF TORTURE

There are three price tags attached to home leave. First there is the cost in cold hard cash. This tab can run exceedingly high depending on where you are posted. In real dollars, you may actually spend little on airplane tickets and hotel reservations along the way, because for some expatriates, they are the typical perquisites of overseas life. Costs run high when you run head on into conspicuous consumer consumption. Heads will turn as you buy two dozen of everything you need, maybe will need, or don't need at all but you haven't seen any of whatever it is for a year.

Before our first home leave from our posting to Bangkok, my husband and I jointly decided that we really didn't need anything and would devote any spare cash to what we really needed – a good time. This, to us, meant movies, restaurants and live entertainment. Given the size of my family (it's true, his family is small; it was all *my* fault we had no time to ourselves) we were able to get to maybe one movie during a three-week leave in Toronto.

But then we decided to visit Toronto's Eaton Center, three levels of what amounted to everything we both absolutely had to have. Did someone drug us? Why did we suddenly pull out our charge cards and start hyperventilating in shoe stores? The sheer volume of available goods simply overwhelmed us. I've known people who have damn near fainted from joy in a K-Mart. The thought of everything one needed under one roof was simply too much to handle at one time.

Also at work is what can be called 'belligerent' spending habits, the kind of mass buying hysteria in stores prompted by an inner voice which says to you: "I'm enduring enough hardships overseas. I want this. I'm going to buy it. I deserve it." Belligerent spending is curtailed only by your credit card spending limit. Ask any expatriate home leaver about the cost of their trip, and they'll tell you they are still paying off their charge cards six months later because it made sense to buy a crate of everything.

And that's just the unnecessary spending. If you're posted to the Sudan or any country where food is limited, you truly are forced to blow your grocery budget a year in advance. The problem is your husband's pay-cheque still only comes twice a month. There is a lot of sighing over the unavoidable hidden costs of home leave such as rented cars and eating out in restaurants.

The other two price tags on home leave – the emotional and physical costs – are not as easy to add up. Unlike credit card receipts, you can't just safely stash them away and total up the damage later. These costs nibble away at you every hour you are home, overlapping and fueling each other. .

The physical exhaustion of flying thousands of miles across ten or twelve time zones often makes emotional crises even harder to handle. You burst into tears because some family member isn't being sensitive enough to your new life, but it could be that your crying is just from being jet-lagged and/or from sheer fatigue.

Or you feel alienated from friends and family, people who mean a lot to you, and blame it on them instead of recognizing that even on returning home for a short period of time, you may be experiencing a bit of reverse culture shock. Your own culture seems strange for a while because you've just finally gotten used to the one over there and now this one seems strange.

Confused? Of course you are. You can get caught in a bit of a culture warp and momentarily lose your balance. You feel as if your brain has been drained of its life sustaining fluids. You feel horribly distracted. You can't seem to concentrate or focus your thoughts. It's easy to throw blame onto your family because – why not? We blame family for everything! In this instance, give them a break. It's nobody's fault. Relax and watch television and ease back into it.

THE NEUTRAL ZONE

Where to stay depends a lot on how long you choose to stay. Will it be just a few days? A week? Longer than two weeks? For just a couple of days, it *may* be all right for your emotional health to stay with family, depending on the size of their house or apartment, and your relationship with them. If tension already exists for whatever reason (they hate your husband, they hate your in-laws, they're not keen on you), better take a pass on the old family dwelling.

If you plan to stay in one metropolitan area and branch out, the smartest thing you can do is to take over some vacationing person's house, or rent a summer cottage. Apartment hotel suites which are cheaper than regular hotel rooms offer weekly rates and a kitchen.

The point is to have your own territory instead of being at the mercy of anybody else. *You* are the one traveling thousands of miles and living out of suitcases. Having neutral territory means you can invite, without guilt, all the people you want to see to your place, all at once or separately.

A good way to see people you don't necessarily need to visit privately is to invite them *en masse*. If it's your own place, and you're doing all the work, then you're not guilt-ridden about heaping burden upon your hosts.

If you're traveling with children, staying put in one place is also better for their mental health and routines, instead of bedhopping across the country or a city. Consider your disorientation, and then think how a three-year-old feels if he wakes up in the middle of the night in the fourth bed he's slept in that week.

Be ready for the tidal waves of guilt which will come crashing around you from disappointed friends or relatives who are absolutely inconsolable that you've chosen to stay in some strange hotel or cottage. But measure that guilt against your angst when by day three, you're ready to slit your wrists and move out. In my opinion, some parents are secretly relieved when visiting expatriate children stay in neutral territory.

Before I forget to mention it, be sure to rent a car. Do not rely on friends and family to chauffeur you around. A car can mean freedom for everyone.

WHAT TO DO?

The short answer is, try not to do everything. The goal of home leave is to lead a reasonably normal life in your old culture, to become reacquainted with friends and family, and to remind yourself of where you come from and your own culture's values and way of life. You can't do this if you schedule visits, appointments, or embark on an endless round of dinner parties every waking minute of the three weeks or so that you are home.

Learn to say no. I know this is hard for some people, myself included, but declining invitations which aren't absolutely necessary means you have the time to relax.

Schedule time for you and you alone. Taking the time to browse quietly in a shopping center instead of being in a constant state of hyperactivity, can do a lot for your mental health. You may also avoid buying frenzies if you're not rushing around like a maniac. I sat in my old public library and read back issues of newspapers and magazines and felt wonderful.

There will be practical issues to be addressed so don't forget to make appointments with dentists and doctors. It's often best to have some family member line those up before you even come home since many doctors are booked months in advance. Make sure you check in with any professional looking after financial affairs for you, or your lawyer. Face-to-face meetings with the people in charge of your life's affairs should be done while you are home, to save on long distance phone calls later.

Use the phone as much as possible, especially if you are unable to visit someone living too far from where you are. Visiting people is important, but visiting places can be equally significant during home leave. Walk down your favorite street and remember the sounds and smells of home. Hang around a main street and listen to the conversations. Take time to read the newspapers and local magazines to catch up on your own country. If you are traveling with children, make sure you do something special for them. Children will not tolerate endless visits to nameless relatives. I've heard of some permanent expatriate American families who make a point of doing some historical sightseeing on every home leave to ensure their children get to know the America they've never lived in.

WHO TO VISIT?

I should really turn this question around. Who should you invite to visit you? For the key to a successful home leave visit, is to make sure that you aren't the one trundling miles out of your way and exhausting yourself to visit someone who could more easily have visited you.

Always accommodate yourself first. That could mean scheduling visiting hours. You are the one spaced out and distracted and exhausted and trying to fit too much into too short a period of time, with lead weights (if you have young children) attached to your ankles. If a friend or family member is unwilling to appreciate the distance you have traveled and all of the mitigating emotional factors, then they are not worth seeing anyway.

Balance each obligatory visit with something fun. Combine visits with entertainment or other points on your home leave wish list. Meet friends and go to a movie or a club or whatever you wanted to squeeze in. Meet at a museum coffee shop or art gallery. Try not to meet at too many restaurants or you'll need to buy new clothes before you return abroad.

THE HOME LEAVE DIET

Laugh if you will. This may be the most important piece of advice yet. Just like you can't do everything, it is also impossible to eat everything. You will be tempted. On my first home leave, I simply could not pass a delicatessen without stopping. It became an obsession. On a home leave from Beijing, Caesar salads became the object of my eating. Learn to say no to a piece of cake or buy a wardrobe the next size up. If it's at all possible, make every attempt to lose five pounds *before* you go home. This serves the dual purpose of giving people the opportunity to say you look great because you've lost a few pounds, and giving you the flexibility to eat your way back up the scale. Despite the stress of arranging home leave and fighting with your spouse, try fasting for a week before leaving.

Try to avoid airplane food. It is not critical to your health to eat four meals in ten hours, so try to eat only one meal and avoid the empty calories of alcohol. If you are traveling with your children, resist the urge to polish off their trays as well as your own.

Feeling fat is never pleasant, but you can still eat wisely and at the same time enjoy all the food you've missed for the time you've been away. Eat in moderation and don't overindulge. Be true to yourself and go ahead, face that mirror, keeping your self-image and self-worth firmly in your mind.

Naturally you can't get regular exercise on home leave, but you'd be amazed how much energy you expend packing and unpacking, dragging luggage through airports where trolleys are non-existent, helping your hostess vacuum and keep her house clean out of guilt, doing laundry for the first time in a year, walking back and forth through shopping centers dazed at the plethora of goods and so on. Many calories are also burnt off in hysteria and family burnout.

So relax about eating. You are not gaining as much weight as you might think, despite all that cake. And remember: you can also lose it anyway when you return to your post.

THE ERRANT HUSBAND

Worse than doing a home leave on your own, is doing it with a husband who takes a powder the minute you hit his mother's house. Look out for one particular warning sign: he brings his golf clubs along.

I've heard too many tales of woe from expatriate wives who have gone the distance, only to find there are more hurdles to overcome once the journey is half done. Understandably, many men have to check in with headquarters, and often get roped into 'temporary duty.' This can't be helped, and should be expected.

Like your life overseas, however, a battle can easily brew over whose leisure time matters more, and what exactly constitutes 'leisure.' If you find you're back to those 'work-related' golf games, let the shouting matches begin.

Make sure both of you know the parameters of each other's free time. You are entitled to time alone as much as he is, and shopping for household goods and children's clothing should not count as your leisure time. Going to lunch, for a walk, to a movie...that's 'alone' time. Make sure you get some and he doesn't hog it all. Remind him of his share of household/childcare duties.

TAKE YOUR MAID

Opinion is divided on this issue. Certainly if you think you have a potential errant husband, it's worth some consideration. Financial restraints may throw the entire question out before it requires any thought at all. But if it's feasible, here are a few pros and cons.

Pros: If you're traveling with small children, having a built-in baby-sitter can't be beat. It means you can see everyone, and not be at the mercy of asking relatives to – heaven forbid – do you a favor and mind your child for the evening. It also takes a lot of stress out of long-distance flying when there is someone else to help amuse the kids for twelve hours. You also get over jet lag faster because a maid/amah/ayah/nanny whatever, lets you catch up on your sleep. When your husband stays behind and you go it alone, a helper could save your life.

Cons: Arriving home with a 'servant' will spark endless conversation from family. Never mind that the people doing the teasing have had live-in help since the second their own children were born. The fact that you've arrived with this foreign woman means you've become a memsahib. You can easily tell these critics to stick it you know where.

More of a problem is the maid herself. You've plucked her out of her own country and you want to be sensitive to her culture shock. You become her lifeline, and that is suffocating in the already choking environment of demanding family.

Her health, what she will eat, the clothes she may need for the new climate: all of these are considerations you must not overlook. The best advice is to rely on your own instincts that you know your maid best and should be able to gauge how she might fare as a traveler.

I am able to share my own positive experience in this area because we took our Thai maid around the world with us when my daughter was just one year old. Our maid was one of those no-nonsense dynamic types who admittedly drove me crazy at times, but whom I would never worry about for an instant on a long trip. She handled the entire experience beautifully, allowed us the clear time to purchase our first home in a matter of days, and gave us the freedom to have a quick holiday in San Francisco at the end of our home leave, by staying put with our daughter in the hotel while we raced from movie to movie to cram it all in.

Best of all, I felt safe on our entire journey because being a devout Buddhist, our maid had a 'blessing ceremony' before we departed. She brought food offerings to the monks at her temple (I told her to buy whatever she needed) and they said special prayers for our safety.

POST-HOME LEAVE BLUES

You think you're depressed about your weight? Your family? Your marriage? All those things which drove you crazy on home leave including the fact that you think your own country is going to the dogs? Wait until you get back to your posting and experience post-home leave blues. It can often be as bad as post-partum depression if not worse. But you do get over it!

Depression upon return is not always immediately felt. First of all, you are so happy to be back in your own home, with privacy again that often the relief you feel is almost intoxicating. This feeling lasts for about forty-eight hours. And then it hits you.

We're really back. To stay. For long-term expatriates, unlike rotational people who leave a place every two or three years, this depression can be particularly bad. Expect to feel it, because not unlike any emotionally intensive experience, you will feel let down when you come home. If you've been back on home leave to a developed country, a return to a less-developed Third World city will be harder. Things will look less organized by comparison. Work hard at reminding yourselves of the pleasures of overseas life. If that doesn't work, think about living full-time near your family.

Most of all, get active again. Don't hang around wishing you were home. Jump back into everything, as soon as possible. The feeling will pass, usually at the same time as your jet lag.

OPTIONAL HOME LEAVE

Is it written down in your contract that you have to actually go home on your leave? If it isn't, and the air tickets and hotel reservations can be used elsewhere, why not alternate home leave with interesting holiday destinations instead?

When we were living in Bangkok, and needed a Western environment for a break, we chose to go down under to Australia and New Zealand instead of going home to Canada. Admittedly, we didn't see family on that holiday, but we did soak up that Western ambience we were missing without the emotional hassles.

Or instead of going home and returning straight back to your post, schedule a holiday somewhere new on the return portion. Incidentally, this option works best on the return. Going home, you're excited and want to get there straight away. Coming back, you often need to stop and decompressurize your brain.

We stopped for five days in San Francisco after our first home leave and managed to do everything we weren't able to do in Canada – watch television, go to movies and restaurants, even read for longer than twenty minutes without somebody offering us a piece of cake. It was worth the extra expense. Likewise, returning to Beijing after a month in Canada, we rested our mouths (from talking, we still ate like crazy) in Vancouver. It was a nice transitional phase and allowed us to get some last-minute relaxation time.

IF IT'S SO BAD, WHY DO WE DO IT?

I hate to get existential about this, it may be positively jarring after my cynicism, but whenever I've asked people in the throes of a torturous home leave why on earth they are doing it, the shrug of their shoulders suggests the same answer an exhausted new parent would give to someone asking them why they bothered to have children.

We go home for some of the same reasons we choose to marry and have children. It's part of the life cycle which somehow can't be denied. In the expatriate life cycle, the urge to return home and touch base with the people we love, and the culture which has shaped our lives just can't be helped.

You know it won't be easy, but it pays to also know what to expect – and what *not* to expect – from the people and places you are going to see. So go with your eyes open and hope for the best.

Chapter Nine

GUILT AND RESENTMENT:
The Expatriate Couple's Extra Baggage

"In a marriage overseas, what else is there besides guilt and resentment?"

Though I was supposed to be asking the questions, that one was posed to me by an American expatriate wife living at the time in Taipei. To an outsider, she would seem the type of woman who successfully adapts to overseas life. Extremely outgoing and talented, she appeared to be living a full professional life abroad while simultaneously raising three children under the age of nine. At the time I spoke to her, she was working full time at a variety of writing and communications jobs in addition to being a major volunteer force in the local foreign community. In the few fleeting uncommitted moments she had in her overloaded day, she confessed her fantasy was a simple one: she dreamed of having time for herself.

Though her question to me had been purely rhetorical, it wasn't too different from the number of similarly cynical and resigned responses I had received when surveying other women for comments on how they handle burning resentment and guilt – the components of an emotional time bomb which ticks away for the duration of many couples' overseas assignments. These feelings are especially intense when a husband has brought his wife and family thousands of miles to an unfamiliar land and then taken a powder from all responsibilities, except his career.

My Taipei friend used many words to describe this not uncommon expatriate phenomenon in which women cope with the battle between their negative emotions – bitterness, estrangement, shame, remorse, alienation – and the positive feelings of the love and ambition they also have for their spouses.

But in the final analysis, most of the conversations I initiated on the subject came down to two words: *his fault.*

"Overseas," my friend said, "men simply resign from family life." And: "I never expected that my husband wouldn't be there to help raise his family...He's never home before eight at night, and often has work to do on weekends...He's too tired for us to entertain friends but there's always time for business."

"Is there hope?" I asked my Taipei friend. "I don't know that we'll ever work it out. He feels guilty and I feel furious."

And then she laughed. "This hell is here to stay," she joked. "So I better have a sense of humor about it."

"WHAT FRESH HELL IS THIS?"

Dorothy Parker, the witty American writer – and one time expatriate herself, albeit in the glorious days of France in the 1920's – was reported to have posed this query in response to a ringing telephone. Many decades later, her famous *bons mots* could easily be adapted for the modern day expatriate wife. What fresh hell and potential emotional danger lies in store when her husband signals the start of his conversation with the words:

"Dear, you may not like this, but I have to...(blank)... (blank)" Substitute with one or more of the following:

(1) go out of town for a two-week business trip right after arrival;

(2) work late tonight at the office/embassy/refugee camp;

(3) take a client out for dinner and you're not invited;

(4) take still another client golfing both Saturday and Sunday;

(5) drag you to a cocktail party I know you don't want to go to/ask you to give a dinner party you don't want to give;

(6) miss taking the kids to their doctor's appointments even though I promised I would because I have to work on an important presentation;

(7) inform you that you won't be able to work at that job you wanted so much because the host government won't allow it/the embassy won't allow it/the company won't allow it;

(8) take the car for the next few weeks while some client is in town;

(9) cancel the holiday we planned for just the two of us, because some important honcho from headquarters is arriving;

(10) send you off to do home leave by yourself with the kids because I can't get away;

(11) move us to some other godforsaken place because that job will be even more wonderful for my career and/or worth a lot of money to us.

Overseas, these and other similar scenarios can always be counted on to provide a sure-fire spark for igniting major confrontations, involving heavy salvos of guilt and resentment. The wife will seldom emerge victorious from such showdowns. Or happy.

Let's examine each one separately. Then you'll have no excuse for saying you didn't know what you were getting into.

But first, let me provide one caveat to this discussion: I will be describing the worst case scenario. Nobody could be as bad as some of the husbands who will crop up in the following pages, although I've personally run into many who come perilously close. Still, I plan to offer a few consoling words in the husband's defence, including one point which should be stated at the outset: many men behave abominably because their wives allow them to. Some women don't raise a fuss until it's too late.

ON THE ROAD AGAIN

You've barely unpacked the boxes when your husband returns home from his new office and announces he has to go away for a few days or even a few weeks. He makes it clear there's no choice involved for him, and furthermore, he warned you there would be travel involved in this new job so don't look so surprised.

Sure you heard about this before you left, but back home you still had all that excitement pumping through you, and your friends and family were nearby. Now that you've arrived in a foreign city, the news stuns you because you just didn't expect the issue would arise so quickly. You're barely over your jet lag. School won't start for another week. You haven't even met anybody yet other than the hired domestic help, except possibly one neighbor you already sense is worried you're going to be a pest. The slow burn begins. What do you do?

Not much, I'm afraid, except to hit him up for as much spare cash as possible (since you're buying everything to settle into your new home and don't want to run short) and to secure a list of emergency phone numbers so you don't feel completely cut off in his absence. Steel yourself for his departure (which can often be that same evening) and tell yourself you're a big girl. And extract a promise from him that upon his return, he'll be obliged to give you some free time to come back down to earth. If he leaves without making such a promise, proceed to unpack all the moving boxes except those containing his clothes, books, games, etc. and leave it for him to do. Hide his sporting equipment and tell him the movers lost that box. And plan your first getaway.

I HAVE TO WORK LATE, DEAR

This will be an on-going problem. The trick is to set certain conditions under which he is positively prohibited from working late (and thereby once again missing the hectic supper/bedtime 'zero' hour around your house if children are involved). Show some flexibility except under the following circumstances: birthdays, anniversaries and other special occasions; particularly bad days for yourself which may coincide with the maid/amah/ayah's day off; and most important of all, *never* allow him to work late when *his* relatives are enjoying your hospitality in one of those month-long travel extravaganzas in which an in-law refuses to leave the house without you. In those cases, he should be forced to arrive home earlier than expected.

I don't intend to delve too deeply into serious marital problems which arise overseas (such as philandering with the local girls which is unfortunately becoming more and more common and messy) but when there have been too many late nights, it may be time to visit his office and gauge the office staff's reaction to your presence. Extreme embarrassment – nobody will look you in the eye – should be your first clue that all is not kosher. Until there's something to suspect, give him the benefit of the doubt that he is indeed working hard. And if you really want to give him a hard time about it, try to have a single good-looking male neighbor from upstairs chatting cozily with you over a drink when he finally does arrive home. That will get his juices going.

WINING AND DINING CLIENTS

An important client is in town without his wife and your husband is responsible for his night-time entertainment. Working suppers at the hotel are one thing; a tour of every sleazy strip joint your city may have to offer is another kettle of fish. These late night jaunts are often critical to the signing of a deal, so it's futile to put up too much of a fuss. The only practical piece of advice I can offer was something suggested to me by a business wife in Taipei whose husband was on the late night social whirl while she stayed at home wondering if he would make it home alive after a night of heavy drinking: Make sure he doesn't drive. If it means hiding the car keys that day, or foregoing a driver so he can work a late shift, the only comfort you can provide for yourself in these instances is to ensure his safety above all else. And put other worries to the back of your brain.

In some cases, your husband may tell you that wives are definitely not on the invitation list. Later, you find out that half the office staff was there, including that exotic, young, unmarried, locally-hired secretary you've had bad dreams about. OK, maybe you are being paranoid, but after too many of those evenings, I would simply arrive uninvited and pay the consequences. Just because you're paranoid, doesn't mean you shouldn't be.

WEEKEND ROUNDS
OF 'WORK-RELATED' GOLF

This is a particularly thorny issue with men. How thorny? When I was living in Taipei, I was asked to write a column for spouses in a magazine produced for the local chapter of the American Chamber of Commerce. I chose the subject of golf.

"There's a four-letter word which is driving women crazy," I wrote, "and it doesn't begin with the letter 'f'. It ends with it." Very funny and well-written was the reaction from the director at the time. "But," he said, "there's no way we can print it without offending our members." Censored.

In my mind, golf is a leisure activity, no matter which way you swing the club. Strolling leisurely down a fairway and stopping for beers afterwards beats dragging the children through a chaotic traffic jam to the local swimming pool for lessons and then watching while a half dozen playmates trash your house all afternoon in an effort to keep everyone occupied on a non-school day. That's invariably the wife's Saturday afternoon scenario while the husband 'unwinds' and talks business over a casual round on the links.

I'm not advocating a complete ban on weekend sports, since they obviously promote good health, mental and physical. But the rules of fair play should be applied to the domestic situation. Set limits on the number of rounds per month. You are allowed leisure time too. Weekends – and all those family amusements – should be shared overseas because they are often difficult to get to, if they even exist.

FORCED-UPON SOCIAL OCCASIONS

"Just this once, dear. I don't ask for much." He's begging you to go with him to a cocktail party where you know with complete certainty there will likely be no other females (or very few) and nobody will be speaking English.

"Forget it. Absolutely not."

A two-hour argument ensues which naturally you don't and can't win. So you go, only to discover that there are no other females and nobody speaks English. You turn right around and walk out the door, ignoring all attempts at an apology. You let the phone ring and ring when you get home and let him sweat about your safety. It takes you about twelve hours to let the resentment ooze out of your pores.

Second scenario: Dinner for twelve people – twelve strangers connected entirely with his work – who would sure love some home cooking since they've been on the road for a while. You have to do all the main cooking but your maid/amah/ayah is still needed in the kitchen and can't possibly be spared for child-related duties. There's still so much to do, especially as you have had less than a day's notice to prepare. The children need to be bathed and put to bed before the guests arrive. Who could possibly be free to handle that task?

Your husband arrives home early enough but: "I have to

have this report read by tomorrow," he whines, "and this time before the guests arrive will be my only chance. Can't you put the kids to bed, dear?" "Is that before or after I ruin the dinner?" If that doesn't work, I suggest immediate strike action. Let him make his own dinner party – at a restaurant.

DOCTOR DISASTER

In some overseas assignments, a simple visit to the doctor can become a complete nightmare. Never mind that half the time, you're unsure of the competency of the local medical profession, to say nothing of abrupt bedside manners which can leave you convinced you're dying of some unnamed (or garbled by a heavy local accent) disease. Just getting to a hospital can sometimes require half a day's commitment. Finding a parking spot when you get there takes the rest of the day.

In short, hospital or doctor's visits can be a nightmare. And just for once, you'd prefer either some help with the expedition, or possibly the opportunity to turn the responsibility over to your husband, who has only heard second-hand tales of the experience.

Emergencies are never planned but inoculations are, and so they lend themselves to a sharing of responsibility towards appointments. Knowing well enough ahead of time when the third injection of whatever childhood vaccination it's to be, means your husband can clear the time well in advance to take junior to the doctor.

But no. The day arrives. No regrets. Either a barefaced lie: "You never told me about this appointment," or a dodge: "Something important has come up." In either event, your blood pressure is boiling. Might as well see the doctor yourself while you're there. Next time, write down the day and time of the appointment with your lipstick all over his best shirt or car windshield. Remind him that the children have two parents and one of them is consistently too busy to look after them.

CAREER DISPUTES

Of all the issues which breed resentment overseas, the pursuit of career goals by the female half of an expatriate couple runs the highest risk for on-going battles and bitterness. Even those woman who are pursuing so-called mobile careers can work up a good sweat over this issue.

What causes a woman's career resentment? It's frustration. It's not a question of salary, as most work obtained overseas by a traveling wife rarely yields high enough money to pay the grocer. More probably, it is a wife's resentment that she is wasting time professionally, or sheer frustration at trying to do anything which is not fraught with hassle because it is being attempted overseas. Add to that some of a wife's own guilt about being out of the work force – and perhaps even enjoying it when she's not frustrated about it – and you find a woman looking for a good fight.

Women want to work for reasons other than money, many of which I explored in chapter five. It is often more than a desire to ensure she doesn't lose track, literally, of her place in the professional world she has chosen for herself. Some women simply do not want to go brain dead if they can help it. Working provides stimulation and the opportunity to enhance oneself which raising children, as cute as they are, just doesn't offer completely.

It's challenging enough to find work overseas which is stimulating and compatible with a woman's skills, so when a husband puts the rein on her efforts, very often for absolutely and purely selfish reasons ("I don't want you working...I want you at home with the children. They need you now that we're abroad"), the wife's resentment levels can cross new thresholds. Don't they need a father, too? you'll likely ask to no avail as he heads for his office.

If you want to work, and your husband is holding you back without good reason, you may have very serious marital problems brewing which can only be alleviated by constant communication and re-evaluation of your life together. If it's alright for him to be compulsive about his career, than you are allowed to be, too. If it's an embassy or company, or the government of the foreign country you are temporarily residing in which is holding you back, it's a serious problem. Short of your husband changing jobs, you're out of luck – and the job market. Try to be mature enough to take such obstacles in your stride.

But worst of all – and worth screaming at the top of your lungs over – is the husband who patronizes your initiative, or displays a lack of understanding about any efforts you may be making on your own professional behalf. There you are, working independently on some life-long project (a book perhaps?) or freelance consulting at anything possible and your entire working infrastructure may depend on maids to do translation, phones which don't work, dangerous taxi rides to get to an appointment, or lengthy waiting periods for minimal payments. And there sits your husband, in a fancy local office, with staff coming and going to arrange all his appointments, drive him to them, and other office support systems. Go ahead. It is hard not to resent him. You're not alone in feeling that way.

It's difficult to rise above these feelings, but you must if you are to go the distance of the posting together. Your working environment will not be the same as his and the sooner you realize this, the less frustrated you will feel. Remember that you don't need to answer to some idiot back in headquarters on the other side of the world. That's just one of your husband's headaches and by all means, leave him to it.

TRANSPORTATION TRAUMA

Getting from place to place in some foreign cities can often be the most formidable problem you face. Traffic jams and overcrowded buses are a familiar sight. Many women enjoy the security and luxury of drivers while others slog it out behind the wheel themselves or take their chances with taxis.

If you get used to the safety and sanctity of a chauffeur-driven car, it will throw you into a panic when your husband informs you that you will have to go without the car while some out-of-town big shot enjoys your perquisite, especially if it coincides with the week you've made several appointments for yourself and children. The office will always take precedence over you, remember that, and that is one reason why from the very beginning, transportation should be negotiated between yourself and your husband.

Try not to agree to use the office car and driver for personal use since this will invite (and rightly so) interference and changes to plans. Try to secure a vehicle which is your own to drive and can't be challenged. If that is not feasible economically, then budget for taxis and buses and learn well in advance how to use them.

If you blindly agree to use only the office transportation when it's convenient, you can be sure that on the day you need it desperately, it won't be available to you. Sure you'll resent your husband, but it's really your own bad planning, and laziness. This is one area of resentment which can be avoided.

ABOUT OUR HOLIDAY, DEAR

You've waited and waited and now you're just hours away from a weekend getaway – just the two of you. It's been so long since you were alone together you can hardly remember the experience. The children have been briefed, the help is in place, the reservations made...and he phones home from the office and calls the whole thing off in a matter of seconds. The boss needs him because some last minute visitor from headquarters has arrived in town.

"I need you, too. We need to get away," you say. "Sorry, maybe next time." He hangs up the phone. You throw yours against the wall. The same thing happens several months later – for almost the same reasons. The boss has some mystical hold on your husband (and his career) and cannot be antagonized, not for your sake anyway. Hold your resentment and anger. Your husband is probably feeling so guilty about canceling that his emotions alone are enough for your marriage to handle at one time. There will be other weekends. However, if he consistently cancels, tell him you're going away with the cute guy from upstairs and see how much the boss needs him.

HOME LEAVE ALONE

To some expatriate women, the shock would probably kill them if their husbands *did* in fact come home with them. They are so used to traveling around the world alone with children and parcels and luggage, and crying on airplanes from exhaustion, and fighting with in-laws from tension and on and on…that if their husband has promised to come along one year and then cancels at the last minute, it will likely be taken in stride along with the rest of the emotional traumas I just described.

I have learned from living overseas to have little or no expectations about anything. That way I avoid intense disappointment. Home leave – alone or with a partner – is definitely one of those areas one should always be prepared to grit one's teeth over and steel one's emotions against in the face of an onslaught of family, food, and fatigue. In this way, if your husband takes a last minute powder, your health doesn't suffer. You're already a mess just from the thought of all that psychological terrorism.

But when you are actually cruising at thirty thousand feet over a major body of water with two children who refuse to go to sleep no matter what medicine you pump into their bodies – that's the time to seethe with resentment and anger. Take a deep breath and remind yourself that everyone gets through it somehow and that it's only once a year. And then conveniently forget to buy him what he wants.

POSTING TIME AGAIN

If anything can be learned from my tales of guilt and resentment contained in this book, it is this: when your husband says you're on the move again, experience should provide you with the information to ask intelligent questions about the next stop on the expatriate express.

Start from the first section and work your way downward. For example, if his working late or too much fuels your resentment, make sure you know how much the next place will require his presence at the office late at night. Devise a point system for the ten areas I highlighted, and if the score runs too high, as in ten out of ten, where the situations will be a nightmare again, then use your common sense and refuse to budge. I am always willing to help soothe any woman's distress if she accidentally walked into the situation which is causing her so much anxiety. But if she knew in advance just how perilous the situation was going to be, she has nobody to blame but herself if she agrees to move again.

In Beijing, I became part of a women's support group (some of the husbands called it the 'women in trouble' group in a complete misunderstanding of its purpose). One subject which roused heated conversation and debate was the option for traveling women to simply say no to their husbands about yet another move or to have veto power over the choice of world capital. I fell into the camp which decided that not only could women say no, they should positively refuse to agree to a move they know will be dissatisfying for them. There are no absolute answers and readers can hold their own arguments over this issue.

IN DEFENCE OF THE MALE SPOUSE

Yes, in the interest of fairness, I am going to attempt to offer a defence for expatriate husbands starting with a reminder that upon your arrival, your husband is tired, jet-lagged and culture shocked just as you are. With input from my own husband (I couldn't have thought up the following rationalizations entirely on my own), I am going to momentarily give the expatriate husband the benefit of the doubt. This exercise should serve the dual purpose of showing what a fair-minded woman I am, and also assist overseas wives in critically assessing their resentment. It also allows me the opportunity to throw cold water over any argument a man may raise in his own defence.

I'll begin with the most important consideration. After reading all of the issues I've just raised which can cause resentment to grow overseas, ask yourself this question: Do many of these same issues happen at home, too? Or have they suddenly cropped up in a foreign country?

Corporate animals – living and breathing by the words of the Chief Executive Officer – do not suddenly appear after a long flight overseas. They often take years to develop and were likely around back home. The same applies to compulsive foreign service officers, and other professions which can totally consume a male spouse. Because of this, many wives should not be surprised when they move abroad and find their husband has become a maniac about his work. If he is working long hours overseas, he probably was doing that same thing before you left to live abroad. A wife should not blame her husband for changing overnight, when she may always have been living with a driven workaholic. Problems of marriage do not vanish when you change location, although many people would like that to be so and move in an attempt to accomplish just that.

Of course back home, where you understood the language, where the infrastructure was solid, friends and family provided support systems, and you yourself may have had a professional identity and well-paying job, it was a little easier to let your husband be driven by his career ambitions.

Defence Number Two: It is a fact that for many expatriates, overseas life often provides such perquisites as servants to help with children, drive you around chaotic cities, and keep your yard clear of leaves or other rubbish. Many households, depending on where you are posted, have enough servants on hand to make sure the expatriate couple do little for themselves at all but enjoy the overseas life.

When a woman starts resenting her husband's long working hours, naturally he will remind her of just how much staff she has at her disposal or how his work is the very reason you're all overseas. He'll push his guilt, if he has any, out of his mind about habitually missing the supper hour with his children because after all the maid is there to do everything. Why should his wife complain? he'll say to his friends.

In situations where servants are affordable and easy to come by, it is indeed true that servants carry a great load for expatriate couples. I mean, why should anyone bother to fold a shirt and put it away when it can be left in a heap on the floor where one drops it, to be washed, ironed and neatly tucked away in the drawer? That may have been all right for the male imperialists of the centuries gone by, but the twenty-first century is almost upon us and the formerly serving classes are now part of the new emerging industrialized nations of the world.

Many expatriate husbands who are essentially the lord and master of their kingdoms at work with local staff members doing everything but kissing their rings, conveniently lose sight of this global view. They abdicate all family responsibilities to their low-paid serfs in the mistaken belief that servants still serve as surrogate parents, which was often the case in the colonial days.

In the diplomatic service, when a man starts taking himself and his inflated overseas position too seriously, it is believed he is suffering from 'Ambassador Syndrome'. A man starts to seriously believe that he is, in fact, His Excellency, and manual labor, like giving his son or daughter a bath, is too much beneath him.

His Excellency must simply be reminded from time to time that back in the real world where he comes from, he is simply Mr. Ordinary Joe and his serving minions will vanish the minute he leaves his job, along with his money (or foreign passports) to hand out. He'd better remember how to do things for himself, because if he doesn't, he may not have a wife and family on his return.

A third defence for the expatriate male: the foreign culture can be blamed for turning him into the monster you claim he's become. This argument definitely has more validity than the other two I just mentioned. It is hard to say no to a local counterpart whose culture – towards women at any rate – may lag centuries behind your own. It's true that many of us come from societies where there are expectations of equality in the raising of our families which just don't exist in other cultures. Japan is a good example of a highly industrialized country in which men spend about as much time on their families as a woman spends in the bath each day.

An expatriate man may be trying to satisfy his clients who expect behavior similar to their own, in which case a man is literally caught between a rock and a hard place. Any way he turns, he is bound to annoy either party. He can risk saying no to his company (usually at the risk of his career) but he can rarely say no to a client. A wife has to understand these cultural and corporate parameters and curb her resentment and anger if she can.

BUT GIVEN ALL THESE EXCUSES...

Despite the pressure being placed on the husband by his work – the *raison d'être* for your life overseas – there are many steps he can take to alleviate some of the resentment they encourage. It's often up to the wife to suggest the following...

(1) Together, you and your husband must designate time each day for each other (and not just saying goodnight). For instance, a husband can leave fifteen minutes later for the office in the morning to allow for a cup of coffee together where nothing controversial is discussed. Talk about anything else, future plans, the weather, a book, but make time for each other and communicate.

(2) Make a date for lunch once a week or a dinner out together alone one evening where you face each other across the table without the distraction of other people or children. Nobody is allowed to cancel.

(3) If you can't get away on a trip, a local hotel room can be booked overnight with a baby-sitter back home allowing you a quiet night together and breakfast alone in the morning. These twelve-hour getaways have proven most effective in many marriages.

(4) Try not to let situations get too inflamed before sitting down to hammer them out. Often, women are their own worst enemies in letting situations slide until they are too far gone. At the first sign of confrontation, get it out in the open and clear the air.

(5) Plan your own private retreat with other women or by yourself, to a spa, a famous tourist site, or perhaps a professional development conference being held regionally. These solo trips are critical to your mental health so make sure you do them when an opportunity presents itself.

All of these suggestions are not beyond the realm of possibility and should be attempted, especially when you live overseas and the day-to-day tension of life in a foreign culture diminishes your powers of patience.

RESENTING YOUR CHILDREN

Feelings of resentment towards your children are much harder to own up to. It's not likely you'll be sitting around with a group of women openly confessing that you wish your children would just vanish for a few days. These are secret resentment scenarios, a natural by-product of life overseas. You feel guilty if your children's health is endangered by poor medical facilities, or a polluted environment; resentful if child-care does not measure up to the quality you may have enjoyed at home.

I'll be the first to admit to resenting my children at various times. When we first arrived on our posting to Taiwan and my son was barely two and so culture shocked he pushed me close to the edge of my sanity, I was constantly torn between my unconditional love for him and my fantasy of walking out the door and doing what I wanted to do, instead of baby-sitting a shrieker.

Day care was invented for a certain kind of mother and I would be lying if I didn't confess I am one of them. I need to have my days to myself to pursue my own interests and career goals. I can't hide this fact. Like a lot of women, I'm also torn between the magazine fantasy of a superwoman and my own reality.

I believe it's natural to have these feelings of resentment. While I don't suggest you tell your children this fact outright, I've had long conversations with my daughter and even with my young son about the direct relationship between mommy's mood and mommy's chance to have some quiet time to work. I find it mutes some of my resentment towards them and at the same time, subliminally teaches them a few life lessons for later. We all need our own time and space – and that includes mommy. The challenge is to come face to face with your child's needs, and work your way around them without resentment and blind fury getting in the way. It took many months, but I finally dealt with my feelings by accepting them and decided to let each day unfold by itself. Some days I could work, others were just impossible. When those latter days arose, I just faced up to it and spent the day at the park.

The guilt you may face by bringing children to an unhealthy environment is another issue altogether and one which is much tougher to reconcile. It also fuels fights with your husband because of course it is *his* fault that you're living in a country which gives your daughter asthma or whatever the local disease may be.

When we moved to Taipei, my daughter spent almost three months with a nagging, phlegmy cough which made her sound like a heavy smoker, which at age six, she definitely was not. The local doctors dismissed the cough with the typical diagnosis: it was the cough all foreign children got because of the pollution. In my daughter's case it wasn't, but we only discovered this after we medically evacuated her out to Hong Kong and saw a specialist. It turned out she had a common allergy, not unlike one I suffer from, and we were able to set her on course. Naturally, I instantly blamed Taiwan for giving my daughter the allergy, until the doctor patiently explained she was going to have it anywhere regardless of where we lived, although polluted Taipei did not improve it.

Your children are going to fall down with many childhood diseases regardless of where you are living, so it's pointless to feel guilty over the bad health. If they do fall down with something which the local environment is most definitely making much worse (asthma for instance) then it's fair game to make sure your husband works fast at moving you out of there. But don't feel guilty over something you can't possibly control.

Another guilt trip endemic to moving children around the world, especially teenagers, is the feeling that you have taken them from their friends and believing them when they shout at you: You've ruined my life! Children will in fact do this, and quite naturally know which guilt strings to pull. In these situations, wait until six months have gone by and your child is truly settled. Chances are they will have found so many new friends that memories of the old ones begin to fade. The long-term advantages you are giving your children by moving them around the world will eventually outweigh adolescent outbursts.

AND NOW FOR THE REAL GUILT

A more straightforward guilt which will be easier to pinpoint, will be the guilt you feel should you be posted to a poverty-stricken country in the Third World. While you are busy complaining about drivers or maids or the quality of the curtains in the family room, outside your gates, women and children are living a marginal existence in some moth-eaten shelter with barely enough to eat. Those husbands are not out working long hours – they have simply vanished, often into prison or a faraway province in search of work, leaving the mother to raise their six children by herself without any support system at all. And of course, without any financial resources except her two strong hands.

Have I made you feel guilty yet? You should, so count your blessings every day of the week. I'm not trying to trivialize all of the preceding discussion about what a creep your husband can be, but when you take time to compare your situation to the desperate lives of half of the world's population, a new perspective dawns on your own 'problems.'

Remember that you are traveling to see how the other half of the world lives, and often it is not a pretty sight. You are insulated and protected with an expatriate life. Whenever you think that life is letting you down, look out the window. And pack up your extra baggage – guilt and resentment – and channel that energy into helping the people with whom you are sharing the scenery. You'll see how quickly the guilt and resentment will vanish and perhaps in the process, improve someone else's life, even just a little bit.

— *Chapter Ten* —

GOING HOME:
Return Shock

The shock of going home will depend a lot on how long you've been away, but absolutely everyone, regardless of the length of their posting, will feel some jolt from the changes to her environment. That is the nature of any kind of adjustment period, and forms the essence of what has now been identified by researchers as 'return shock': the adjustment period to unexpected changes in the people you knew, the places you lived, the events you have missed; and the unexpected changes in yourself, both emotionally and physically.

My first re-entry experience after three years in Thailand offered me its share of jolts. The biggest shock of all was feeling like an outsider in my own culture. While I lived in Bangkok, I was used to feeling like an alien because I was one; in Canada, I should have felt right at home but instead I felt totally disconnected and left out of the mainstream. My cultural reference points were out of date. I had nothing current to contribute to a conversation: the biggest shock of all for a constant talker like myself!

One of my strongest shocks occurred at a Blue Jays baseball game. The cheering crowd jumped to its feet to execute the 'wave.' I thought it was absolutely wonderful and unique and couldn't stop laughing until my companions regarded me strangely with that "Where've you been? Outer Space?" look. I took my seat, the smile wiped from my face. I would barely venture another cheer and chose instead to stuff my face with mystery meat hot dogs and doughy pretzels. It felt like I had really landed from Mars, not the Far East. I didn't just feel completely out of it. I was.

The good news in this scenario, though, is that like its counterpart – straightforward culture shock – it is not fatal. You get over it, especially if you can laugh about it, and not just in a hysterical, over-the-edge kind of way. You do eventually catch up on people and events, even though you may continue to draw blanks when certain years come up. It truly helps, though, if you know what to watch out for.

THE CHALLENGES OF RETURNING

Some expatriates positively fear the idea of going home and avoid it at all costs, especially if they think they might return to home base and never get out in the world again. Foreign service people are luckier: it's usually part of their rotational life to be returned home for a two or three-year assignment before taking another posting abroad. Knowing it is part of your international life cycle, means you can build contingency plans into the routine, such as owning a house back in your own country which allows you to take up residence in the same neighborhood each time you're posted home.

Returning to your own familiar neighborhood can help soften one of the major shocks of re-entry – the strain of stepping back into a strange setting in your own country.

Unlike your posting abroad, there will be no Community Center or built-in support system waiting to brief you on local life, prices and culture. You're expected to know these things. You're from that country after all, even if the neighborhood is new and the absence of support groups can make you feel extremely isolated at the beginning.

Traveling and living in a country profoundly different from your own, can't help but alter your outlook on life. You may look upon your old institutions and organizations with a new perspective which isn't always very positive. We tend to idealize our country when we're away, and when we return and find our own society riddled with problems, or unappreciative of just how well-off we are compared to other countries, it tends to encourage cynicism and bad feelings all round.

You want to shout at your old friends and neighbors that they are exceedingly well off. They look at your outbursts askance, and then carry on complaining about the price of a recreational vehicle. So you may regard your friends in a new light which may not be so glowing. They've changed, too, but you feel your change has been more dramatic, leading to a tendency to dismiss anything which may have happened in their lives. Once again, you feel alienated from your old circle of friends and acquaintances, and feel even more disconnected from your new home environment.

Family can pose another problem, especially if an aging parent has been looked after by a sibling who looks at you upon return and says: "OK, now it's your turn to look after mother. I've done it for three years and I'm taking a break now that you're back." You feel barely capable of organizing your own family's life, and suddenly there is filial duty beckoning.

Careers may be re-evaluated by your new, internationally enlightened persona. I made a complete career change upon returning to Canada from Thailand. Before I left home, I had been a broadcast journalist. When I returned, and unpacked my old television clothes (which admittedly after the birth of my daughter couldn't fit over my expanded body) I instantly threw them in a pile for the Salvation Army.

I felt those clothes fitted a woman who just didn't exist anymore. I looked at myself critically in the mirror and did not see the former television reporter staring back at me. Far from being tailored and professional looking, my hair was wild looking; I'd toned down my makeup almost to nothing since I had been permanently tanned from the tropical Thai sun, and my glasses (previously horn-rimmed academic-looking frames) were now bright pink. Who would possibly hire me now, I thought, except a traveling circus? Granted, I fell back temporarily into the more anonymous radio service (I had to make some money, after all) but I knew there was no going back to the kind of professional television person I used to be.

Children are especially vulnerable when they return home, and require more than the usual attention in order to settle into new schools and new routines. They, more than you, will have to cope with cultural ignorance, such as not knowing the current television shows, pop stars, or cartoon hero. If they are entering junior or senior high school, when peer pressure to conform is at its greatest, their feelings of alienation can set off all sorts of adjustment problems and depression. Your husband, too, may need your support and common sense to see him through the transition. The changes in his working environment and status may easily unravel him in the beginning.

As the wife and mother, you must deal with all of your family's issues while simultaneously unpacking, decorating, stocking up, renovating and a thousand and one other responsibilities which in combination will give you sleepless nights. Your own life is put on hold until you get your family settled and that may depress you if you're anxious to get onto something new. Still, as many are the challenges to re-entry, so too are the number of solutions, which I will deal with later in this chapter.

THERE'S NO PLACE LIKE HOME

Before getting down to the challenges one by one, however, I feel it's important to stress that while many negative factors will be at work during your first months back, there are also many positive feelings to be savored. Certainly there will be drawbacks to being home, but don't forget for one minute the advantages – and sweetness – of being home.

The day we drove up the lane to our house, soon after our return from Thailand, through the pine trees, past the duck pond and up the hill to where our house sits on a wide open meadow, fronted by a panoramic view of the Gatineau Hills outside of Canada's capital city, Ottawa, my breath and heart literally stopped. It was so beautiful. There was barely a sound other than the wind; a clean, sweet-smelling wind to distract us. Wild flowers were blooming around the house and in the meadow. The grass (we hadn't seen real grass in years) was freshly cut in a fringe around our acre of land. I wanted to cry I was so happy to be home. I was also so relieved that we hadn't made a mistake in buying so swiftly, I wanted to kiss the wild flowers.

It's true we sometimes tend to falsely idealize our home countries during an overseas assignment. Exasperated by an alien environment and climate, we delude ourselves into thinking there's no place in the world as clean, as organized, as crime-free, as poverty-free, as picture perfect as our country of birth. It's wrong to paint such a false picture without running the risk of complete disillusionment when we return home. But at the same time, there's no law against truly cherishing and certainly not dismissing the small things that can make going home such a moving experience.

RE-ENTRY IS A THREE-STEP PROCESS

Think of your return home as an experience which will have three distinct stages. The first obvious step will be to let go of the past. This is known as the 'closure' stage. You are not only closing up a house or apartment at post, you are closing up your overseas life as well. It's crucial that you feel like you have physically closed up shop as it were, in order to know that part of your life is truly over, leaving only memories to linger in your mind – not deeds or goodbyes left half-done. For that reason, make sure you say all your farewells. Don't disappear out of town. Try to do all the things you never got around to doing, like visiting a spectacular tourist site or museum. Allow your children to say goodbye completely by scheduling sleep-overs with friends, or organizing their own farewell parties at school or at home.

Try to get everything done within four days of your departure so you can relax and take a few deep breaths before heading out to the airport. Similarly, try not to mentally leave a place too early. If you have moved in your mind three months before your physical departure, that can be unhealthy as well. Try to balance out your time doing something each day until your departure date while allowing some quiet time before beginning the long trek home. Being organized helps. Don't worry that you have lists all over the place. Do what I did before moving abroad my second time. I pasted notes all over my house with the words: "DON'T PANIC" in every room to keep myself from hyperventilating.

The second stage is the turmoil, or crazy period when you're neither here nor there. It's part of the process of disconnecting and can bring with it feelings similar to the anger and depression you felt when you first went abroad. You're out of control again. Perhaps you're 'home' but living out of a suitcase, camping out in a parent's spare bedroom or hotel suite.

This is the unsettled time, when the previous life has ended, but the new one at home hasn't settled into any recognizable pattern as yet. You may still be traveling, or at home renovating and fixing up your house. Your days are filled with checking out new schools, activities for toddlers, buying new cars or furniture, or attending to the million and one details of moving into a new environment.

The long trip back to your own country may be behind you, but there are still many miles to go mentally until you have truly arrived home. Think of this stage as one of uncertainty. Don't expect instant routines. Give yourself a break emotionally and don't expect too much too fast. Rome wasn't built in a day, and all those other clichés which always contain a kernel of truth in them.

The third and final phase of the re-entry process is the period of reconnection. The house is liveable again, your furniture has arrived, the kids are back at school and finally you have a minute to yourself to think about what you may want to do.

I remember so clearly when this phase struck home for me on my first re-entry. My then two-year-old daughter was settling into a new baby-sitting situation; the house had furniture even if more pieces were required. My husband had returned to a headquarters job and I sat in a shopping mall enjoying a coffee, that day's morning newspaper (not one three or four weeks out of date) and a glorious bran muffin, something I hadn't tasted in three years.

The satisfaction I received from the bran muffin alone came close to euphoria. I wanted to cry I felt so happy to be back in Canada. Never mind that I didn't know what I was going to do. I enjoyed the fleeting moment of satisfaction of being home just as the leaves were changing color, the air was crisp, and the unpolluted sky was the brightest of blues.

THE ISSUES YOU WILL FACE

Still, when the bran muffin was eaten, the coffee drunk to the last drop and the newspaper read from cover to cover, I was faced with a reality not unlike the 'now what?' syndrome I described in an earlier chapter. Just as I had to get on with my life overseas and not mope around, now I was back home, I had to get on with my life again, and together with my husband, there were issues we had to face head on and could no longer postpone.

FLYING MONEY

Your foreign money, the kind whose exchange rates seemed as enigmatic as the people on the streets back at post, goes into the drawer for future trips. The time arrives to confront the new budget. Sure, you started to think in your local currency the moment you stepped off the plane, but now the bills are being totaled up and both you and your husband can no longer avoid the complete and horrifying fiscal panic of being home.

While fixing up our new house on our first re-entry, I had joked with my husband that our money had taken wing and could be seen soaring over the hills of our new panoramic view. It was flying at a fast and furious pace. Appliances, carpets, cars, day care, groceries, warm clothes...the expenses went on and on. So did our 'budget discussions,' usually in an atmosphere so tense we could have marketed it for a new form of energy. We were horrified at the new controls we had no choice but to impose on our lifestyle. We had a mortgage for the first time in our lives, taxes, and all sorts of hidden costs to home-owning no one could possibly have prepared us for.

Watching money fly is a popular post-expatriate life game, except no one is enjoying it because in the real world there is no cost-of-living allowances which allowed you that fantasy life back at post. Nobody is helping you adjust to your new high cost of living now, and the price of everything – and everything you need to buy at once – reduces you to many, many stormy sessions with your spouse. You can't complain to anyone because your friends figure you've made a fortune overseas and lived the good life long enough.

The best you can do under your new restraints is draw up a budget not unlike the Western governments. Set priorities on your needs and expectations for the coming year and allot existing funds, what may be left of your savings, to those needs. Make sure your budget is based on sound price surveys. Be realistic. You can't cut yourself off from life completely. It would be as extreme as going on a 700 calorie a day diet.

A DECISION A DAY...

Another popular game for returning expatriates is called decision-overload. How many critical decisions can you try to make in a single day? Sometimes there can be so many decisions to be made at once that you spend as much time deciding on a new car, as you spend on selecting a salt and pepper shaker.

Decision-making can't be helped on re-entry. In your hurry to get everyone settled and some semblance of order restored as quickly as possible, you want all the pieces of your new life to fall together in the fastest possible time. This encourages hasty decision-making, and lumping too many crucial decisions – ones you would normally take weeks to make – in the space of hours instead of weeks.

New furniture and cars seem to get quick nods from a lot of returning expatriates. Under normal circumstances, price surveys, consumer reports and other information gathering would be done. Not so in the case of a returning family. Research flies out the window, as does good taste. Be aware that this could happen to you and put the brakes on the minute you feel yourself playing the game too much in earnest. A half-empty house filled with furniture you like, as opposed to ugly stuff you picked out too quickly, will be a happier home in the end. The same applies to a car worth its money. Take a deep breath and try to look before you leap.

NO SUPPORT SYSTEM

For those who had servants while overseas, you will feel a kind of panic erupting when you realize the servants you relied on overseas didn't come home in the shipment. How can I manage my household, you wonder frantically, forgetting you did it for many years before enjoying the luxury of servants, whom you have conveniently forgotten drove you crazy. I was so relieved to be servantless on returning to Canada, that I joyfully cleaned toilets and vacuumed away my first few weeks. I can't guarantee this feeling will continue, but the point to be made here is that you're not as helpless as you think. When you moved abroad, you were also well taken care of for the first weeks after your arrival by another company wife, or embassy official, or perhaps a professional orientation organization. Your questions were answered, sympathy was ministered, and emotionally you felt there were others in the same boat as yourself and you took comfort from that.

The absence of this life support system on returning home can at first leave you feeling helpless and without resources. It's true it's jarring, but getting used to your own country all over again will not be as hard as adjusting at post, even if it seems formidable at first. After all, people speak your language at home. And friends, who may have momentarily been distracted by the new you will come around. They are your friends. Don't be afraid to ask them for help.

YOUR CHILDREN'S SAFETY

Overseas, your children were never far from your watchful eye. At home, suddenly they want to hang out in the local mall with their pals, or ride their bike in the street. As a mother, your heart goes into your throat at the thought of their new-found independence which they couldn't enjoy at post.

It's natural to find these fears bubbling to the surface when you re-enter your old society. How you control them will be up to the individual, but at least acknowledge those fears will be there – and some of them for very good reasons depending on the city you return to. But you can't tie a rope to your children, especially if they are teenagers. All you can hope is that the good sense you ground into them will prevail.

HOW NOT TO BUY IN BULK

I heard a wonderful story of an expatriate returnee whose first grocery shopping trip, to fill her cupboards with staples and such, produced a whopping bill when she finally managed to steer her shopping carts (yes, carts) to the checkout counter.

Examining the high price of her goods, she realized she had bought dozens of everything, instead of the typical amounts one normally would buy for a week or two.

She was still in 'home leave shopping mode' – that frenetic, grab-it-all, load-it-up style of consumer madness normally associated with home leave, when you buy as much as possible at one time in order to last you several months overseas.

You're home now. All those goods will continue to be stocked on the shelves at reasonably stable prices. There's no need to stockpile in case of famine or siege. Make a list before you go shopping and reasonably assess your family's needs under the new conditions. Another good idea when re-balancing the grocery budget under returnee austerity programs is to make a list of each night's meals for a week or two and buy only what you'll need for those lunches or suppers.

The same control should be applied to department stores. No need to buy two dozen cotton undies at once, or a year's supply of expensive makeup. You can go back to the store again.

SERVANTS

I've known expatriate couples who claim they can never go home again because without servants to pick up the pieces of their lives every day – meaning their pieces of discarded clothing – their marriages would fail to survive more than a day. For some couples, this fear is not totally without grounds.

Men get used to having constant help not only to assuage their guilt over running off to the golf course every weekend, but to keep their wives happy without the burden of cleaning toilets. Women get used to having a jack-of-all-trades handy in the house to do everything from baby-sit to sew a button back on a jacket. And let's not forget all that ironing! For their part, children enjoy having a 'neutral' third party to run to in the event of disagreements with their parents.

If servants have been used as day care, family budgets will also have to be re-adjusted in order to cope with the shock of finding out what day care costs back home. How you adjust to a servantless life will depend a lot on your personality. In my own case, I was relieved beyond belief not to have servants hovering in my background, quietly manipulating me into decisions, making me feel completely useless as mother and homemaker, and leading me into scores of other emotional traumas I've worked hard to forget. This is not the case for everyone. If your return home with toddlers is to a four-bedroom house which needs a lot of cleaning, be prepared to have the most exhausting of return shocks. You'll become Molly the Maid in suburban wherever, trapped within the walls of your house, mop in hand, tears rolling down your face from the exhaustion of re-entering the domestic labor force.

If you are returning home to a 'servantless' society remember that there are people known as cleaning ladies; there are cleaning services which can be called in once in a while; there are home day care centers; and there is your husband, whose job at home may not call him away as much nor require his presence every evening at a cocktail reception. Before you get totally overwhelmed by your new domestic lot, negotiate a new agreement – a living at home, not abroad agreement – with your husband. And then place an ad in the local paper for the cheapest available help.

On the other hand, those returning to home countries where servants are plentiful will feel the sweet relief of having help once again, to peel, slice, chop, cook, mop, sweep, clean, wash, iron, baby-sit...Once again you will be able to enjoy waking up late, knowing that the breakfast is already prepared for the children. The laundry will all be done, ironed and neatly kept away, you won't even have to handwash delicate lingerie yourself anymore. All the hassles of hiring good help and training them may go unnoticed when you first come home because all you can think of is that now someone else will be doing the chores you had to endure overseas.

EXTENDED FAMILY
You may think fondly of family when you're overseas and separated by expensive long distance phone lines and mail which takes weeks to arrive, but your feelings can change dramatically when that same extended family is just round the corner or in the next town. All of the decisions and feelings

you've been able to defer while being away, will now come crashing around you, just at the time you need it the least – when you're in the throes of return shock. Your own problems of readjustment will seem insurmountable, but load those up with the problems of a sibling about to get divorced, or an aging parent who requires hospitalization. Or just consider all the petty problems endemic to any typical family: the kind that will really make your blood boil especially if you've spent the last number of years in a poverty-stricken country. You will easily lose patience with family members complaining about their suburban neighbors who have an annoying dog, an unpainted fence, or uncut grass which your sibling complains is the blight of the neighborhood.

Patience is a virtue. I've said it before, I'll keep saying it. Your family simply does not understand where you're coming from (truly) and will be impatient with your limited interest in these so-called major problems which you just can't get excited over.

Aging, ill parents on the other hand, are serious problems you can't fly away from anymore so be sure to preserve your best frame of mind for dealing with these more important issues. As for the rest of the so-called ills, try to laugh about them without alienating everybody. Don't engage in futile arguments where you glaze everyone's eyes over with statistics of starving children or politically repressed adults who would give their lives to live in neighborhoods with uncut grass or half painted fences. It doesn't do anybody any good, especially you. You're trying to reconnect with your family – not distance yourself even further.

THE BOREDOM FACTOR

Where have all the interesting new people gone? Where are the fascinating visitors, the exotic side to life, the opportunities to see something you've never seen before, or heard before? One of the major reasons a former expatriate will decide to return to the international life, is the feeling that there is no excitement in sitting home in suburbia, watching the grass grow (only to be cut). There is a certain excitement to stepping on an airplane, passport in hand, flying off to an unknown destination and facing the challenge of carving out a fulfilling life for yourself. There may be no such opportunities once you've moved home. You may feel, not long after you've settled in again, that you're itching to get away again. Many people do just that. They find another assignment and put this returning home idea on the back burner for another decade.

But if there's no option – this is it, you're home – it's at this point when the initiatives for participation and enthusiasm must be undertaken, even if at the beginning, your personal campaign to get excited is a little forced. It's the flip side of when you moved overseas and were advised to seek out opportunities – social and professional – as quickly as possible. The same ambition must be mustered back home. Nobody will hand you excitement or a new opportunity. The chance to branch out, even within a community you thought you knew inside out, exists if you know what you are looking for. Cultural societies abound in most cities, you may never have been looking for them before. Universities may offer courses related to the country you've just lived in. Antiques, art, music, ballet, theatre, museums – all of these art forms and institutions may be out there to offer points of contact if you are interested in keeping your mind open and satisfy a craving to learn more about the country you just left. But you won't find it staring out the window of your house into a deserted street.

THE HUMBLED/ELEVATED HUSBAND

Once you've got yourself or your children out of a return funk, you'll likely be left facing your husband's let-down on being back at headquarters. His mood can affect the entire family. Overseas, he may have been riding high on his own self-importance to the point you wanted to throttle him once a day. Back at home, you're feeling sorry for him (as he is often feeling for himself) watching him go through the motions of a job which may not offer a tenth of the excitement and glamor which his overseas assignment gave him. Instead of strutting out to work into a shiny, overseas corporate office, or valiantly heading the evacuation of flood victims in a remote village, he is standing on the bus clutching a strap with his briefcase held tightly between his knees. It can be a pathetic sight.

However, a good position back at headquarters may be a reward for a job well done abroad. If it's not, you can remind him (as often as necessary) that while overseas jobs can be glamorous and challenging, it is typically from headquarters that promotions and careers are often made. Overseas, people tend to be forgotten, even if they are having the time of their lives. Your husband needs to be back home for a while to network with the top men, or just the ordinary middle men who may hold the keys for future challenges. So while he may feel humbled momentarily, in the long run, he is doing his career a service by being back in the heart of the action, whether it be corporate or government.

In contrast to the humbled husband, your husband could have just returned from overseas after successfully completing his doctorate or an intensive training program. He returns home to discover that he has status now he's only dreamed about before. Most probably, he will be promoted and receive a much higher salary. Friends, neighbors and relatives may even regard him with awe. You become the mate of a man whose feet have left the ground. Pull him back down before he floats away on a cloud of prestige.

HOW NOT TO BE THE MISFIT FAMILY

There are obviously many things you should bear in mind when you are returning home from overseas after a long period. Here are a few more pointers on how to smooth out the transition from living overseas to living back home.

Plan Ahead

Some experts on the 'return shock' syndrome believe that planning for your return home should be started when you first move overseas. Obviously, it's difficult to think of coming home before you've even left, but you can do some planning, such as buying a house – or renting your own house – to make sure you and your family return to the same neighborhood. At your posting, there are a few measures you can take as well. One precaution we took against believing our own Raj-like lifestyle in Bangkok was driving our own Canadian car. I suppose it's terrific if you can afford a luxury car and driver, but remember that when you go home again, it may be back to economy cars again. Try to keep a clear head on your shoulders. It will make it easier when you go back to your real world.

Temper Expectations

Expectations can be deadly. Don't get it into your head that your home base will be perfect because it won't. Sometimes it's particularly easy to fall into this trap if you haven't really enjoyed your overseas assignment. You convince yourself that back there at home is some suburban utopian crime-free society.

As I mentioned earlier, I had a horrible experience just prior to my return to Canada from Thailand which shook any idealized expectations I had of a safe world back home. One week before my daughter and I were scheduled to fly home to Canada – just the two of us – an Air India 747 was blown out of the sky. The bomb originated in a Canadian airport, as did a second bomb fortunately undetonated in mid-air on a flight headed to the Far East.

So much for thinking home was going to be safe. Expectations about family can also be dangerous. Don't expect miracle reconciliations with family members you didn't get along with before you left home.

Try Not to Re-Enter Alone

My flight home from Bangkok reminds me of another important piece of advice. Try to return home together. Often, this isn't possible, if your husband has work to finish up and you're anxious to grab the kids and be on your way, which was my own experience. Sure you'd love to escape, but getting to the other end and facing all the return shocks can be very hard on you emotionally.

Not only did traveling alone exhaust me beyond belief, but being without a partner with whom I could share all my return shock with – look at that green park, those empty streets, that loud-mouthed politician – was tough going. Unilateral decision-making is also difficult. It may pay to wait a few extra weeks to go home together.

Communicate

Before you leave and after you return, make sure the lines of communication between you and your children are not only open, but working overtime. Take your children to lunch before departure and hear out what they have to say about going home. Listen carefully to their expectations, and apprehensions. Likewise, once you're home, listen to them some more. Don't get so wrapped up in picking out new wallpaper or carpeting that you don't hear them when they tell you they're scared, or tired all the time, or depressed. The same applies to your husband. Make sure you schedule time for conversation in between all that tying up of loose ends. During the chaotic post-arrival home time, try to get out to dinner or for a walk and check in with each other's feelings.

Special Needs for Children

I can't go into all the special emotional stroking your children will need, but I can mention a few areas to look out for. When it comes to decision-making, include your children wherever possible, especially if you are decorating a brand new room for them. Their bedrooms will become a safe haven so make sure it's one they'll enjoy bringing their new friends to. Find new activities for your children as a way of distracting them from their feelings of uprootedness. Sure, new activities require more effort and momentary feelings of alienation. But that is quickly replaced with new friends and new interests, which activities will encourage. Most of all, and especially if your children are teenagers, have a chat with their new teachers about not singling them out to talk about where they've just lived. Fitting in and seeming as normal as possible is a top priority for a teenager, so try to avoid a spotlight being cast on your child as the 'kid who just returned from...' If there is a cousin of the same age around, make sure you bring your children together for briefings on the latest slang, pop stars, cartoons, movies, or any other cultural reference point which may help bring your child up to date and feeling less like an outsider.

See Your Country as a Tourist
Another idea which works at bringing everyone up to date, is to travel within your own country for a few weeks before settling in. This gives everyone a local/national focus again and provides conversation starters which don't necessarily deal with the country you've just returned from. Along the way, watch the evening news shows, read newspapers and soak up the new trends in lifestyle you have definitely missed while living abroad. Appreciate the cultural differences between home and abroad. Sure there were things you probably will miss from your overseas home, but a local tour may help remind you of all the things you hated to leave in the first place.

Find Others Like Yourselves
By this piece of advice, I don't mean that you should drop old friends just because they haven't traveled. But broaden

your circle of friends to include people like yourselves who have lived expatriate lives. You can speak the same language and share your re-entry experiences.

Self-Confidence Returns

Your self-confidence first vanished when you moved away. Now it vanishes again upon return. There's a contradiction at work here. On the one hand, your self-confidence may be overwhelming when it comes to subjects like foreign travel, or the culture you enjoyed while away. On the other hand, you forget how to use a shopping center or call up a maintenance man or speak the local dialect and you watch your mood plummet.

Trying to stay on an even keel in the way you view yourself, can seem a daunting task at the beginning, but it can be done if you expect wild mood swings to occur and plan appropriately. For instance, if you decide to go out and look for a job, don't do it on a day you've just freaked out over your inability to cope with childcare all over again. Wait for a day you can secure a baby-sitter and have a few minutes to yourself before rushing into someone's office all flustered and hysterical. Nobody is going to hire you in that state.

From my own experience, I found my self-confidence level soared when I returned briefly to my old profession as a freelance journalist. What had been unbelievably difficult to carry out in Bangkok, a simple assignment, foiled by useless telephones, transportation nightmares, hassle factors which measured right off the scale, became as easy as pie back home. It didn't matter to me what an editor asked me to do when I discovered I could easily phone someone up for an interview (and an English-speaking person would answer the phone); I could drive to my appointment myself in traffic which was humanly safe; and the hassles were so limited I almost felt giddy.

It Takes a Full Cycle of Seasons

Certainly after six months you will begin to feel like your old self, but some people believe that the full re-entry cycle will take an entire year or four seasons (if you live where there are four seasons). You can also measure this cycle by the major holidays and festivals. You won't feel like you're really home until you've had your first Thanksgiving and Christmas back, your first Easter, May long and July long weekend, New Year's Day, National Day, Independence Day...or any major holiday unique to your own country. When that cycle is complete, you'll know that you've come home.

GIVE YOURSELF ENOUGH TIME

Knowing that the re-entry experience requires a certain amount of time for readjustments will go a long way to easing the transition from over there to over here. As I have been trying to stress throughout these pages, information is power, and the more you know about how you're going to feel (and how other people are going to feel) the more it will boost your sense of excitement and satisfaction over the experience, and that of your family too.

Don't expect too much at once, and don't expect too much of yourself. These are the final words of self-taught wisdom I can offer, except to suggest that you keep this book within easy reach for your next international assignment, just to remind yourself that although it won't be easy, you *can* make a success of living abroad. You will be making the move with an international community of soul mates, and sharing the common experiences of surviving overseas.

RESOURCE GUIDE

WEBSITES

American Women Overseas
(http://www.awoscentral.com/)
This is a 'virtual shelter' assist women who are victims of domestic violence overseas and have no place to turn. It's a secure site which offers women a way of going to it without anyone finding out.

Escape Artist
(http://www.escapeartist.com/)
A super expat site filled with tons of information and an on-line magazine.

Expat Exchange
(http://www.expatexchange.com/)
An on line expatriate community with lots of info and links for expats and repats. One of the first expat communities to go on line.

The Expat Expert
(http://www.expatexpert.com/)
This is my own website for families of the international workforce. There are lots of excerpts from books, opinion and links to other sites.

Expatmoms
(http://www.expat-moms.com/)
A site created by a repatriated expat mom for other expatriate mothers everywhere.

**Expatriate Living
(http://www.suite101.com/welcome.cfm/
expatriate_living/)**
The website of author Huw Francis who is an accompanying
'husband' and has articles on the subject and much more.

ExpatSpouse.com (http://www.expatspouse.com/)
This is a fee-for-service web site for expatriate spouses which
many companies and organizations have joined on behalf of
their relocating families.

**Federation of American Women's Clubs Overseas
(http://www.fawco.org/)**
A complete listing of American women's clubs to help women
find an organization near them. Through FAWCO, you can find
out about other local groups catering to your nationality.

**Outpost Expatriate Information Center
(http://www.outpostexpat.nl/)**
This is the mega-site of Outpost, the family services center
established by Royal Dutch/Shell and available free to anyone
with an Internet connection.

Tales from a Small Planet (http://www.thesun.org/)
This wonderful site, which started out as a subversive e-zine put
out by American foreign service spouses, offers 'real post reports'
written by spouses in-country.

**Woman Abroad Magazine
(http://www.womanabroad.com/)**
The on-line site of a magazine designed for women on the move.

FURTHER READING

Many informative and helpful books designed to help spouses cope with the challenges of successful living abroad have been published since *A Wife's Guide* first appeared. There are far too numerous to give a comprehensive here list but several publishing houses specialize in titles for expatriates. They are Times Publishing (which publishes the *Culture Shock!* series), Intercultural Press and Aletheia Publications.

A Career in your Suitcase, Joanna Parfitt (Summertime Publishing, 1998). Author and journalist Parfitt weaves together success stories and advice from women who have carved out satisfying professional situations while accompanying their spouses on overseas assignments.

Culture Shock! A Parent's Guide, Robin Pascoe (Times Editions Pte Ltd, 1993). Raising happy, well-adjusted children is always a challenge for parents, regardless of where they live. But overseas, parenting issues are magnified because traditional life supports are absent. This is my own book that examines many of those challenges and offer support and advice.

Homeward Bound: A Spouse's Guide to Repatriation, Robin Pascoe (Expatriate Press, 2000). Like the move overseas, the move home relies on a solid and stable person to act as the emotional touchstone in order to help everyone else in the family through re-entry shock. That someone is typically the spouse. Homeward Bound is my own 'repatriation reality check' to help spouses create new, meaningful lives when they return from abroad.

Intercultural Marriage: Promises and Pitfalls, Dugan Romano (Intercultural Press, 1997). Author Dugan Romano examines the impact of cultural differences on marriage and offers practical guidelines on how to deal with the complexities and problems involved. Romano suggests that the joys of an intercultural marriage often result as much from overcoming the obstacles and confronting the challenges as from the adventure of crossing cultures.

The Third Culture Kid Experience, Growing Up among Worlds, David C. Pollock and Ruth E. Van Reken (Intercultural Press, 1999). The authors explore systematically and compassionately the experiences of those who have become known as "third culture kids" (TCKs)—children who grow up or spend a significant part of their childhood living abroad. Rich with real-life anecdotes from TCKs, this is one of the first books to fully examine the nature of the TCK experience and its effect on maturing, developing a sense of identity, and adjusting to one's "passport country" upon return.

Women's Guide to Living Overseas, Nancy J. Piet-Pelon and Barbara Hornby (Intercultural Press, 1992). This perceptive book was written by two women who have lived abroad for many years. In it, they examine issues critical to women and their families who relocate abroad. They also provide sound advice on how to cope effectively with the problems that arise.

THE AUTHOR

Since the publication of *Culture Shock! A Wife's Guide* in 1992 and *Culture Shock! A Parent's Guide* in 1993, Robin Pascoe has regularly been called to speak to expatriate groups and human resource professionals about the importance of understanding the needs of the expatriate spouse and family. Both books address these needs and are widely used as reference by expatriates around the world. She has lived in Bangkok, Taipei, Beijing and Seoul—the experiences she skilfully and with much humor writes about in her books. She presently lives in Vancouver, Canada, and can be contacted at http://www.expatexpert.com/, her website for expatriate spouses and families.

INDEX